If only we could climb the stairway
to heaven,

for one last hug...

Jewish Bereaved Parents Inc.
ABN 16 609 169 280

We are an independent support group
for Jewish parents
who have suffered the devastating death of a child
(whatever age or circumstance).

After the death of your child

A Jewish mother's perspective

By Cynthia Pollak

In loving memory of our darling son
Daniel (Danny) Julius Pollak
דוד יעקב בן מנחם חיים וזלדה ליבה
6/9/1979 – 22/9/2008

Table of Contents

AUTHOR'S NOTE

I am the founder and president of Jewish Bereaved Parents Inc (JBP). We have grown from a small peer-support group in 2011, to a comprehensive organisation providing a range of activities and levels of support for Jewish mothers and fathers who have suffered the tragic death of a child.

My aim is for a copy of this book to be given to every newly bereaved Jewish parent in Australia, through burial societies and synagogues.

The contents of this book are my own thoughts, experiences and feelings. I have no formal training in the field of grief support and in no way do I consider myself a counsellor. I strongly urge you to seek professional advice if you are not coping.

The production of this book would not have been possible without generous support. I am grateful to the rabbis who have encouraged me to write this book, as well as to the Australian Centre for Grief and Bereavement and The Compassionate Friends (Vic) for their support.

I am also grateful to Adele Hulse, who supported me in this project from the very start and whose knowledge and insight have been invaluable.

Thank you to all those who edited and proofread the manuscript and offered suggestions.

Finally, a special thank you to all the bereaved parents who opened their hearts to me. It has been of enormous benefit to me as I hope, has my support been to them.

Cynthia Pollak

Melbourne, 2018

If you would like to contact me, with comments or suggestions for any future reprint, please email me at cynthiapollak@gmail.com.

Additional copies of this book are available directly from Jewish Bereaved Parents Inc (email me), from the Lamm Jewish Library of Australia and, hopefully, from every *shule* and Jewish burial society in Australia.

<u>PREFACE</u>

My mother died of cancer and was buried on Tuesday, 2 February 1999. She was the last of my two children's four grandparents, who all died within ten years of each other.

Three days later, on Friday, 5 February 1999, my nineteen-year-old son was diagnosed with a rare vascular cancer, Epithelioid Hemangioendothelioma (EHE). His condition was described as incurable, untreatable and fatal. When diagnosed he had about twenty tumours, which increased to over 100 before he succumbed. We were told there was no cure and it was not likely there would ever be one because EHE was so rare: one case a year in Australia, twenty a year in the USA. The oncologist bluntly explained, 'Research into it is not worth a share of the world's health dollar.'

These words have haunted me ever since.

In 1999, almost nothing was known about this cancer by the medical profession. (Even now, there is very limited knowledge of it.) There were no support groups and only a few papers had been written on it. But I am a Jewish mother and my child was sick, so I did what any Yiddishe mother would do: I started an international support group and a detailed registry for people with this cancer.

Over the next ten years, I accumulated data on over 350 people worldwide who had been diagnosed with this cancer. I maintained regular correspondence with many of them via email or telephone. My registry included the names of doctors and hospitals, patients' symptoms, treatments, the effects of treatments, ongoing issues and more.

Through the registry I was in touch with scores of people who later lost their battle, and I knew Danny's condition was more serious than most.

Oncologists from around the world requested copies of the registry and it was referenced in several medical papers.   The Royal Melbourne Hospital created an International Database on Rare Cancers based on my registry.

But none of this helped Danny.

Danny's death in 2008 was sudden and, thankfully, in his sleep. He was away from home on business at the time, but I was very aware of his prognosis and had always lived in fear of this inevitable end. He was twenty-nine years of age, married and had an eighteen-month-old daughter.

Danny lived his life to the fullest. I think he lived on love: his love for life, his family and his faith.

Danny attended Leibler Yavneh College for his final two years of schooling (1996-1997) and they had a huge impact on his life. He thrived on *yiddishkeit*[1] and spent part of 1998 in Israel, which helped consolidate his enthusiasm for living a more observant lifestyle. Sadly, his year overseas was cut short when a disorder in his

---

[1] *Yiddishkeit* – the quality of being Jewish, the Jewish way of life and its customs and practices

bones was detected, later diagnosed as multiple metastasized EHE.

For the rest of his life Danny strove to learn as much about Jewish law and observance as he could. He stayed involved with the social group Bnei Akiva for many years and threw his heart into the work of the United Jewish Education Board, deeply concerned that every Jewish child should have access to Jewish education.

Danny was asked why he persisted with his university studies and supporting the community when he had only limited time left on earth. He was asked: 'Why not do what gives you the most pleasure?' He replied that he was doing just that. Danny thrived on doing the same things his friends were doing: spending time with his family and friends, his involvement with Bnei Akiva and community affairs, going to university, and later on, his work commitments. He was adamant that he did not want to be known as 'the cancer boy'. Danny's friends all knew of his health condition, but he never told his university or work colleagues. Yet, for these ten years Danny averaged one medical appointment every single week.

Despite writing his final exams while standing because it hurt too much to sit for long periods, Danny completed his law/commerce degree with honours. He became a lawyer and then a barrister.

Danny married Shelley in 2005. Their beautiful daughter, Noa, was just eighteen months old when her *Abba*, her father, died.

My husband, Peter, and I have learnt a lot about our son since he passed away: about the numerous people whose lives he touched, how much time he devoted to his *davening* and learning, and what an inspiration he was to so many people.

We took great *naches* from seeing the development of this young man we had nurtured, and have always been so very proud of him. But when did our influence finish and his own initiative take over? In adulthood, Danny was indeed his own person, an upright man of strong principles with a steadfast determination to be the very best he could be.

At Danny's funeral Rabbi Fromer said that he did not understand what to 'choose life' meant (Deuteronomy 30:19) until Danny died.

What else would anyone choose when life and death are placed before you? Danny faced such a choice in the way he would approach his life with a terminal illness hanging over him. He chose not to be a victim, not to wallow in self-pity, or to put everything on hold while he dealt with his illness. He chose to fill whatever days he was to be granted with the most that life could offer him.

Danny chose life.

No matter what G-d decides for us, we all have a choice about how we live the life we are granted. May Danny's legacy be that we all actively and consciously 'choose life'.

A young-adult *minyan,* Ohr David, has been formed at the Mizrachi congregation in Melbourne in memory of Danny and uses the Torah donated by family and friends in his honour. The inscription on its cover reads 'And he planted eternal life within us'.

Throughout the ten years I spent watching over our son since his diagnosis, I knew his time was limited and I lived every day in fear of him having an accident, a fall, of being knocked – anything that might upset his precarious system.

After he died I read a lot of books about death, dying and terminal cancer. I read about the range of emotions one experiences, but was not prepared for the loneliness. I felt quite sure that I was the only Jewish person I knew who had lost a child. Yet, in my short street of thirty-two homes, three other Jewish families had also lost a child.

Searching for comfort in books, I soon learned that there are not many in libraries or local shops that deal with the death of a child. I scoured the internet and over time built up a library of over 100 relevant books, almost all published overseas, and just one small booklet that was specifically written for a Jewish market.

When a newly-bereaved mother reached out to me, eighteen months after Danny's death, I was happy to help her. Marina Briskin and I realised the value of being there for each other, and together, we decided to provide support for others who were hurting as we were. With the help of grief counsellor, Shelley Katz, we started a peer-support program, and I thank Shelley sincerely for her wonderful support and encouragement.

However, I felt the need for a more social group with fun activities, where members could 'act' like normal ... until it really became our new normal, and we could rejoin society. Indeed, our members began to feel more comfortable attending these less formal functions.

After five years of managing a variety of activities for our growing number of bereaved families, I established Jewish Bereaved Parents Inc. in 2016. A group of bereaved mothers get together for video nights, exercise classes, Scrabble games, art and craft, lunches and to make items for charity. In the relaxed atmosphere in which we all understand and respect each other, we talk openly and freely.

JBP also provides a support group for fathers, with regular gatherings and *shiurim*[2] where a relevant topic is presented, and where they have a chance to express their feelings with others who understand and share the same experience.

The Jewish Bereaved Parents Support Group operates out of our Quiet Room at the rear of the Lamm Jewish Library of Australia, at 304 Hawthorn Rd, Caulfield South, right beside the Beth Weizmann Jewish Community Centre. This room is available to our members whenever the library is open.

There are couches, tea and coffee facilities and shelves of books dealing with the death of a child, help for siblings and grandparents, as well as support books for parents of children who took their own lives. There are also books for young children whose parent has died. These books are all free for any bereaved parent or bereaved child to borrow.

Like Danny, I wanted to do something normal. I did not want to just sit around discussing how we dealt with the deaths in our families, or how we coped. I wanted us to

---

[2] *Shiur (shiurim*, plural) – a lecture or study session where any Torah subject is discussed.

do what we would have been doing if our children had not died. And along the way, and in our own time, we have many and varied discussions over crayons and Scrabble tiles. Yes, we may discuss our children and our feelings of loss, but we have also learned to laugh again, without feeling guilty or uncaring in the eyes of others.

I try to contact newly bereaved parents in Melbourne, just to let them know we are here. When and if they feel ready, we can meet. Some of these parents get real bencfit from sharing their pain with others undergoing the same experience. Others prefer not to share distressing emotions. We are all different.

__INTRODUCTION__

We cannot, after all, judge a biography by its length, by the number of pages in it; we must judge by the richness of the contents.

Sometimes the 'unfinisheds' are among the most beautiful symphonies.

Viktor E Frankl

My hope is that this book speaks directly to all Jewish bereaved parents, regardless of their stream of Judaism, level of observance or the circumstances of their child's death.

You may not be ready to read this just yet. Sometimes the pain is too raw. Later, you may want to look at a chapter or an anecdote and for this reason I have repeated myself in some sections, so you have the suitable information at hand wherever you open this book. Let this book become your quiet companion.

I cannot stem the many tears that will flow, nor would I try to. Our lives have been shattered and will never be the same.

I know words alone cannot ease your pain, but it might help you to know that there are others who really do understand what you are going through. You are not alone.

It is hard to write about this without being subjective and you may not agree with some of what I write. Your experience may be very different, but this book may help you explore and understand your own experience and emotions.

One bereaved mother, just approaching the first *Yahrzeit*[3], read a small segment of this book as I was writing it and reported back to me. 'I just finished reading your book. I can't believe how you have captured so much. It's made me realise that I am 'normal' and what I feel is ok. It will be invaluable to people who are just beginning this traumatic journey. Wish I had read it months ago.'

I hope this book helps you too but remember that we all grieve differently and there are no right or wrong ways to grieve. Form your own approach and you will grow stronger in the process.

---

[3] *Yartzeit* – the anniversary of the death, observed by the recital of the Kaddish and the lighting of a memorial candle.

WHEN YOUR CHILD DIES

An angel in the Book of Life wrote down my baby's birth. And whispered as she closed the book, "Too beautiful for earth." **Author unknown**

First and foremost, I offer you my deepest condolences. Sadly, I do know how you feel and can understand your pain.

The death of your child will probably be the most devastating experience of your life.

Regardless of how your child died or how old at the time, it seems an irreparable injustice for this to have occurred. We don't expect our child to pre-decease us. It is not the norm. It's not right. It's totally unjust!

Whether your child's death was sudden or anticipated, and whatever the age, acknowledging the full reality of the loss may take weeks, months or even years.

Your heart has been pierced. Will you ever feel whole again? Our comfortable, secure lives have been shattered, our innocence has gone.

As you mourn the death of your child, your agony will slowly subside although it will never fully disappear. How can it? The hole in your heart is still present – but instead of only emptying out, your heart will slowly allow things to enter in.

Often, when recalling the death of a parent, a close relative or even a pet, people say to us, 'I know it's not the same, but I do know how you feel.' They are wrong. No one can really understand another's pain and I am sure no one can come anywhere near understanding the devastation for bereaved parents.

'Why?' is accompanied by 'how?' Why did my child die? How can I go on living?

The only hope I can give you is that I, and others like me, have survived.

As a newly bereaved parent you have experienced a devastating, life-changing event, but life goes on, whether we are prepared for it or not.

There are no words for it – there is no single word for it. If you lose your spouse you become a widow or widower, if you lose your parents you become an orphan. But what are you if you lose a child? What about those who lose their only child? I cannot begin to imagine the grief of parents in this situation, but I can put you in touch with someone in a similar situation if you need to share. You will always be a parent. To become a parent is to open a door that can never be closed.

<u>WHY AM I WRITING THIS BOOK?</u>

Say not in grief 'he is no more' but in thankfulness that he was. **- Hebrew Proverb**

Why am I writing this book? I'm writing this book for you. Do you feel alone, deserted, abandoned? You're not. Unfortunately, there are quite a few others in our community who have also suffered the death of one or more children.

This is not meant to take away your pain, but to let you know you are not alone and there are other parents you can reach out to for support and advice on how they managed to survive and go on living after their devastating loss.

Who am I? I am Renée and Danny's mother. I am Peter's wife. I am Cynthia.

I have worked with computers for almost fifty years, been married for over forty-five years, and a mum for over forty years, yet I still place 'mum' as my primary role – even though the kids left home to get married some ten to fifteen years ago. That's me.

My role as a mother is a very significant part of who I am. When my darling son Danny died, there was a death inside of me too. A part of my heart died.

While writing this book I had so many mixed emotions, yet felt confidant I had the necessary strength and conviction to complete it. I recognised the urgency of offering support to other bereaved parents, but as time went by uncovered more of my own insecurities.

I have expressed both these trains of thought, because we all have mixed feelings. We must all deal with both positive and negative emotions as we make our way through our lives, especially when the script has suddenly been re-written.

This book may not bring you immediate relief from your grief. But I hope it might guide and support you, and help you cope in your new world.

Burying a child stands the world on its head. Everything that we cherished is inverted, back-to-front and out-of-synch. We wonder how the world can have the arrogance to carry on when our own private universe has been decimated. Things don't make sense after your child's death. Your sense of personal and global equilibrium is shattered.

You will not get over the death of your child. But you will go on. You will go on as a changed person, stronger, because you have withstood the ultimate test any mortal can confront.

Did you notice that I do not say 'my late son', or 'Danny z"l'[4]? Because in my heart, Danny is still alive, my memories of him are embedded in me and I am certainly still his mother.

But now I am also able to look forward, to enjoy each day, play with the grandchildren, and appreciate what I do have. Now, when my friends say, 'How are you going', I answer, 'I'm OK' and realise that indeed I am.

This is not a religious book, it's not a guideline. It's the story of my journey and maybe it can help guide you. I am not a therapist, grief counsellor or psychologist – I am a

---

[4] z"l stands for the Hebrew words zikhrono livrakh, meaning 'of blessed memory'

bereaved parent and have experienced the same unimaginable pain you are going through.

The early days after your child's death will be horrible. I hope that maybe if you get a chance to read this in quiet times you might find some strength knowing that others do understand you, and truly empathise with you.

At the back of this book is a collection of writings. When you are ready you may find some comfort in them.

The search for meaning is a very personal journey and no one can tell you how to cope after your child's death. No two people respond in the same way and husbands and wives usually have differing emotions to deal with. My husband and I certainly did.

When you start to venture out of your home you may feel that everyone is looking at you wherever you go. You may be feeling vulnerable. 'Is this normal? I feel everyone is looking, yet they are avoiding me. Why? Why? Do I look different on the outside as well as the inside?'

Slowly, you will re-enter society and find your place among family, friends and colleagues. Your body, your heart and your brain will guide you.

If only we could climb the stairway to heaven,

for one last hug...

<u>DEFINING GRIEF</u>

No one ever told me that grief felt so like fear.

C.S. Lewis

Grief is not an illness from which we recover. Rather, we accommodate and change.

While most of us will move forward from mourning the loss of our beloved child (se*e next section)* we do not get over our grief – we learn to integrate it into our lives. You won't ever move on from grieving the death of your child, but you will move on with your loss.

Grief demands an enormous toll – physically, emotionally, mentally and spiritually. Common grief responses include a range of intense feelings such as sadness, anger, anxiety, disbelief, panic, relief, irritability or numbness. Grief can also affect our thinking. You may think you will never get over this, that you are going crazy or even think you might be better off if you join your deceased child. Grief may cause difficulty in sleeping and physical symptoms such as headaches, nausea, aches and pains. With time, these symptoms will lessen, though the sorrow we feel will always be a part of us. (If physical symptoms persist, check with your GP to exclude other causes.)

The risk factors for experiencing more serious symptoms of grief for a longer period of time, are related to the survivor's own physical and emotional health before the loss, the closeness of the relationship between the bereaved and the child, as well as the nature of the death.

But for you right now, there is no right or wrong (as long as you do nothing illegal). Whatever emotions you feel are normal for you and should be expressed.

Barbara Wiseman, a US obstetrician[5], noted that although trained to deal with the death process, many doctors did not know how to help survivors. When their child died she and her husband, a surgeon, were shocked to realise how little they and their fellow physicians understood about grief. Doctors with no training in grief typically, do not understand it.

At times you may feel like you are drowning in your grief. This may go on for many, many months. It will start to ebb and flow, providing brief periods of respite in the midst of intensity. Gradually you will notice what helps comfort you – it may be to talk to a friend, go for a walk, have a hot drink. It is uphill work, learning to take care of yourself and discover small pleasures.

Bottling up strong emotions is never healthy. It's important that you express what you feel, be it anger, frustration, disappointment, sadness. This may be least risky in the protective environment of a bereavement group.

Ultimately, it is normal to want to live as fully as possible, for our own sakes, and for our family and friends. Perhaps it is a choice – we choose whether to live or merely to exist. We choose to be eternally morose or we strive for the recovery of hopefulness and joy.

One source I came across estimated that parents need to allow themselves a period of one to two years to get to a stage where their grief isn't their absolute centre of attention. This is not 'getting over it', it is learning to live

---

[5] Wiseman, Barbara, MD, Pennsylvania, USA, in an article provided by The Compassionate Friends, 1997

with your altered life. Personally, I found the third year even harder, while some people may find the fourth year the hardest. There are no rules on grieving. Our first year was consumed by numbness, and then anger until we finally fully accepted the reality of Danny's death.

Although your grief will feel less intense over years, it will never completely go away. Just as your child was a part of your life, so are the memories of your child. Your grief must be addressed. It cannot be avoided, ignored or filed away. You must go through it to emerge on the other side. As much as you may not be able to believe it now, your grief will shift and become less all-consuming as time goes by. You will smile and find joy again, but right now, you must follow your instincts and allow your heart, mind, and body to grieve.

It may help to participate in a group with others who are suffering similarly, struggling to stay afloat in a sea of societal indifference and lack of understanding.

The Compassionate Friends, a worldwide, non-denominational support service for the bereaved on which we modelled our peer-support meetings, state: 'Although your grief will be yours and yours alone, know that you are not alone. There are others who are willing to walk beside you on this journey, others who want to help.'

Later in this chapter is a list of some of the feelings you may experience. Not everyone will have these feelings, some will be felt more strongly than others and they may come in any order or be mixed up together. It is also important to note that for most of us these feelings will not last forever, although at times it may seem that the pain will never end.

UNDERSTANDING THE DIFFERENCE BETWEEN GRIEF AND MOURNING

Grief refers to the specific set of cognitive, emotional and social difficulties that follow the death of a loved one, the thoughts, feelings and potentially disruptive aspects of the mourner's day-to-day living following the death.

Mourning can be defined as the conventional manifestation of sorrow for a person's death such as observing the week of *Shiva*.

I grieve over Danny's death, but I am no longer in mourning. There is no choice – I have adapted, sadly, to a life without my son.

Grief refers to the thoughts and feelings you experience, while mourning is the outward expression of grief. Mourning is crying, journaling, telling the story, speaking the unspeakable and adapting to the loss.

Everyone grieves when someone they love dies, but if we are to heal we must also mourn.

Reaching out to others while in mourning can be helpful. Mourning is hard work and you cannot always get through it on your own, though you also need some solitude. Heed the call for contemplative silence, when required.

Take comfort in other bereaved parents. They have something many of your friends do not possess. Sadly, they have experience. They are parents who have learnt to survive.

We must come to terms with what has changed in our lives. There is no 'return to normal', rather, we must learn to live a new kind of normal – relearning the world and relearning ourselves within it.

That does not mean we return unscathed to normal life. The loss will always be there, the future is affected.

For some men there may be a sense of loss in the broken lineage. Children generally take their father's name and the loss of a child may mean the end of the line on the family tree. It is not a major factor, but it must be recognised. As a female, I was oblivious to this and surprised to hear of it from several families. I do remember when Danny was born how happy my husband, the only child of Holocaust survivors, was to know the Pollak name would carry on. But now that won't be happening. Another adjustment.

HOW LONG DOES THE INTENSE GRIEF PROCESS LAST?

There is no predictable schedule for grief and the length of the process is different for everyone.

How long does this intense grief process last? For some people the period of intense grieving can be relatively short. They may have to rush back to work, may be busy with their other children or have other commitments. Others may still be struggling to cope well into the second or third year, or even longer. Sadly, unbelievably, there may be further complications that arise.

It can be agonizing at times and cannot and should not be rushed. It is important to be patient with yourself as you experience your unique reactions to the loss. With time and support, things generally do get better. It is normal for significant dates, holidays or other reminders to trigger feelings related to the loss. This may occur at any time, over an extended period – months, years or decades after the death. Taking care of yourself, seeking support and acknowledging your feelings during these times are ways that can help you cope.

It is important to recognise that grief is not something that will simply go away with the passage of time or a lack of attention to it. No one will be 'done' with grief. By contrast, you will process the grief individually and at your own pace, folding it into your life in a way that becomes more manageable over time.

SUDDEN VERSUS PREDICTABLE DEATH

Sudden death due to unknown health issues, accidents, or suicide are horrendously traumatic. There is no way to prepare for it. It challenges your sense of security and confidence in the predictability of life. And it leaves unfinished business – there has been no opportunity to say, 'I love you' and 'Goodbye'. There may be everlasting regret for all that was left unsaid.

Predictable losses, like those due to terminal illness, sometimes allow more time to prepare for the loss. However, they create two layers of grief: that grief related to the anticipation of the loss and that related to the loss itself.

If your child has endured a long incurable illness – you live in hope, but also with reservations. You expect it to happen, you fear when the phone rings late at night, but it is still a shock when you get that call. After being told my nineteen-year-old son had a fatal incurable cancer, I lived the next ten years in fear. When the time came that Danny failed to keep an appointment, we knew the reason why. I grieve for Danny, but I no longer live in fear.

However, for those living a seemingly blessed life, to be suddenly confronted with the death of their child turns their world upside down from one moment to the next. It destroys their sense of security and permanence and their trust that each day will merrily follow the last. This cruel, devastating shock – the realisation that a life well-lived, a life full of virtue and goodness has not protected them from the very worst thing that can happen – it is an unimaginable blow. Suddenly, with no warning or premonition, an irreversible bullet has lodged in their heart and cut off a part of their own life.

SUICIDE

Modern thinking recognizes that major depression is the most common cause of suicide. A chemical imbalance in the brain is harder to detect than a broken leg or heart disease, so frequently goes undetected. A brain disorder is a matter of biochemistry and genetics. It has nothing to do with willpower, how a person was raised or a failure of character.

Most people who attempt suicide are not acting on a sudden impulse or out of moral or physical frailty; rather, they are engulfed by mental illness which causes unbearable pain, an illness that generates an urge to self-destruction as the only escape from that pain. One parent reported that her daughter had described her unbearable life and her struggles to overcome depression in this way, 'It's like trying to draw a rainbow with a black pen.'

When a person dies by suicide it is commonly said that he 'committed suicide'. This phrase is particularly hurtful to survivors because of the stigma it perpetuates. People 'commit' crimes, deliberately unlawful acts. People are 'committed' to institutions because they, presumably, are unable to care for themselves properly.

These people have not committed crimes. They have taken their own lives out of desperation and feelings of hopelessness. It is terrible enough that they died in this way and we should not allow people to add to the burden, weighing it with a sense that a loved ones committed a criminal act.

It was illogical and wrong, but my husband and I both initially felt we had let our son down, that we were somehow responsible for his death. I imagine that for a parent whose child takes his or her own life, no matter what age, feelings of inadequacy and bad parenting may surface automatically, when this is definitely not the case. It is for this reason that parents bereaved by suicide often have great difficulty expressing feelings publicly.

As you regain a degree of strength and start out on the long journey toward recovery, one of the feelings you might want to express is resentment over the additional and unwarranted insult contained in the expression 'commit suicide.' The most essential ingredient in surviving well, besides facing reality, is to speak of your child unashamedly.

Society blames people for mental illness in a way that it almost never blames people with cancer or other illnesses. The labelling of mentally ill people as 'bad' puts an unwarranted stigma on the victim and his family.

Whether as a response to stigma or out of other personal needs, some people deny that their child chose to take his or her own life. Too often, however, denial stands in the way of survivors forgiving themselves for not being able to prevent the child's death, thereby intensifying feelings of guilt and despair. Denial can change accepting and confronting the unpleasant reality of suicide into a 'nasty little secret' you work so hard to conceal that you end up diverting energy into negative directions. It is hard to say, 'My child killed himself', but it is even harder to live in denial.

You know you loved your child and tried in every way you could to understand what he or she was going through and help him or her. The love and support you offered your child, the doctors and the other knowledgeable people you consulted, the efforts you made to intervene, all demonstrate the depth of your love and caring. While it is natural to feel like you could have done more, and to wish the outcome had been different, you did your very best. You have nothing to be ashamed of or to feel guilty about.

Even if you did not realise that your child was suffering and did not intervene in any way, you must forgive yourself for what you did not know. You loved your child, you did not cause his or her death and you need not feel guilty.

A helpful resource may be a group in which participants have a common bond. A support group of bereaved parents is a good start. The fact is, for all of us, no matter how it happened, our children died and that unites us.

You may prefer a specific suicide support group. In Melbourne, the Australian Centre for Grief and Bereavement (03 92652100) have trained counsellors. The Compassionate Friends Victoria (03 9888 4034), run a monthly support group for parents. Also, Jesuit Social Services (03 9421 7600) provides a non-denominational program 'Support After Suicide'[6], with support

---

[6] https://jss.org.au/what-we-do/mental-health-and-wellbeing/support-after-suicide/

groups for those recently bereaved. I have heard from several of our members that this was very helpful.

When you are hurt it is normal to become angry – angry at yourself and others in the family for what they did or did not do. Perhaps angry at the child for wasting his or her life. It is good to express this anger among those who have 'been there' and truly understand.

Participation in a group with others suffering similarly can provide essential support – initially for your own survival and ultimately, for recovery.

NORMAL GRIEF REACTIONS

I don't need to go into great detail because you will be experiencing some or all of these already, but you can be reassured that these feelings are normal.

We do not always know how people are grieving simply by what we see. Some people are open and expressive with their grief, crying and wanting to talk, while others are more private, may be reluctant to talk and prefer to keep busy.

Grief is a process, a moving through. Sometimes we go forwards but sometimes backwards. Sometimes we get stuck for a while. But most of us do eventually move though the process of intense grieving.

It is a common myth that people 'get over' grief. The reality is that a part of us will always grieve the loss of a loved one. With time, the pain will lessen, but the sorrow we feel will always be a part of us. There is no 'return to normal'. Rather we must learn to live around a new kind of normal, relearning the world and relearning ourselves within it.

How long will it last until we feel we belong in this distorted world? Often two years is quoted, but I don't think that figure has been expressed by anyone who has lost a child. Another reference quoted four years, while a bereaved friend of mine stated seven years.

It was once explained to me that it takes a few years to get over the initial period of grief, and then several years of going through yearly cycles – *Yomtovs*, birthdays, *Yahrzeits*, maybe a family *Bar Mitzvah*, wedding or other major milestone – to reach a new version of 'normal'.

It also depends on many other factors – your personality, your upbringing, the circumstances of the death, your support system and whatever else is happening in your life, together with family, friends and work commitments. For me, it took around seven years to be able to say, with a clear conscience, 'I'm OK'.

Many people say that grief is forever. We just learn to rebuild our lives, find new meaning and a new normal.

Here is a list of the recognised symptoms of grief.

Shock and disbelief

A child is a living extension of ourselves, so the loss feels like an amputation. It is a death of part of ourselves and you will probably react to learning of the death of your child with numbed disbelief. You may deny the reality of the loss at some level, to avoid the pain. Early on, shock provides emotional protection from being overwhelmed all at once. This may last for weeks. Shock knocks some of us into merciful oblivion and you may not remember a thing during this early time.

These feelings of shock, numbness and disbelief are nature's way of temporarily protecting us from the full reality.

Gradually, we come to realize that this is not just a bad dream from which we'll awaken, and the rollercoaster of severe emotions hits us.

Gradually, these severe emotions get easier, but they re-emerge, over and over again. Birthdays, anniversaries and festivals may often trigger these feelings. Sometimes feelings may resurface for no apparent reason. This is normal.

Some parents can never overcome their grief – they do not want to. They are scared that if they stop mourning they will forget their child. Other parents will do anything they can to avoid mentioning their dead child. Yet for me, talking about Danny acknowledges that he lived and keeps his memory alive.

Denial

Initially, denial helps us survive the loss. You might think life makes no sense, has no meaning and is too overwhelming. You start to deny the news and in effect, go numb. It is common to wonder how life will go. You are in a state of shock because life as you once knew it has changed in an instant.

The relationship we had with our child determines how our lives will be uprooted or altered. It is very common for people to try and initially deny the event to subconsciously avoid the sadness, or the thought of the pending mental struggles.

Denial and shock help you cope and survive the death. Denial aids in pacing your feelings of grief. Instead of becoming completely overwhelmed, we deny the grief, do not accept it and do not allow its full impact to fall on us at once. It is as if our body's natural defence mechanism is telling us there is only so much we can handle.

Once denial and shock start to fade, the start of the healing process begins. At this point, those feelings you were once suppressing come to the surface.

Anger and bargaining

Anger is a natural normal reaction to protest the death of your child. Do not be afraid or ashamed of it. You will not always feel this way. You have a right to be angry (but be careful not to take it out on innocent people). It is not chosen. It is not a matter of will or intention.

As with all emotions in the grief process, people vary greatly in their experience of grief, but our anger must be resolved for us to finally accept the death of our child. Unexpressed anger leads to unresolved anger which may lead to bitterness and possibly depression. Our children should be remembered not with bitterness but with love. The feelings we have for our children will be desecrated if they leave us with anger and resentment.

Angry feelings can be compared with taking a deep breath. They cannot be held forever and will not go away until you release them. Anger can take many forms and affect people differently. Some people can openly express their anger, while others are more private and reticent.

Anger needs to be expressed. Even if the words are yelled and screamed, the expression is healthy and therapeutic. Let out your anger – exercise, scream in the shower, do housework – release it any way you can.

Crying can be a release of anger. Listening to our child's favourite music, looking at pictures and doing things that remind us of our child may force the tears to flow. This is a good thing, because it is a natural means of enforcing the reality.

Anger needs a target. It may be directed at the doctor, the hospital, G-d, someone else, yourself, or even your deceased child. It is a defence against accepting the new reality.

Sometimes we express our anger at innocent people. I remember at one of our *minyans* a rabbi offered condolence to my husband Peter, and Peter furiously argued back, 'Life will never be the same, why did G-d let this happen?' This rabbi, not from our regular shule, understood our anguish and has indeed become a strong pillar of support for us. He was so considerate that eleven months later, as we were on our way to Danny's consecration, he remembered and rang from Israel to wish us long life.

Anger is a natural human response. We don't choose to be angry, but our anger serves as a protest and we hit out at whatever we can – at those we think contributed or caused the death, at ourselves for letting it happen, at G-d for having abandoned us.

In the bargaining phase you may find yourself intensely focused on what you think you could have done differently to have prevented this loss. You may try to bargain in vain with G-d for a way out of your despair. 'I promise to be more observant, I will go to *shule* regularly if you just bring him back.' This may be a time when our faith in G-d is severely challenged.

Pain and guilt

As shock and denial wear off, they are replaced with the suffering of unbelievable pain. Although excruciating and almost unbearable, it is important that you experience this pain fully and not hide it, avoid it or escape from it.

Pain is an acceptable guest, but not a welcome long-term visitor. It will never completely disappear – to let it do so would be to forget, and you will never forget your beloved child.

Bereaved parents may torture themselves with unhealthy irrational self-destructive guilt, based on faulty reasoning. You may have guilty feelings or remorse over things you did or didn't do with your beloved child. Life feels chaotic and scary during this phase.

For some ridiculous reason, I was convinced that Danny developed his rare blood vessel cancer because I never insisted he ate his chopped liver on Friday night. My husband was convinced Danny acquired his cancer because my father-in-law had bowel cancer.

Danny had full blood tests before he went to Israel for his gap year. No abnormalities were detected, despite the fact that he probably had harboured this irregularity for at least four years, if not from infancy.

Danny endured ten years of the best medical help, yet it took months until we stopped blaming ourselves with these absurd, senseless, baseless suppositions.

Many parents feel guilty about one thing or another. They may feel guilty that they did not stop their child from driving at night, did not take the child to the doctor sooner, were not perfect parents. Feeling of inadequacy may rise, doubting ourselves, undermining our self confidence and parenting skills.

Yes, for some the thought of taking our own lives is considered because the pain is so great - and we will be with our loved ones. This is definitely not the answer.

You loved your child. The extent of your mourning shows this. Do not hide your feelings of guilt. Discuss them with family or friends, a support group or professional and watch their power diminish.

Depression, reflection, loneliness

Just when your friends may think you should be getting on with your life, a period of sad reflection will likely overtake you. This is a normal stage of grief, so do not be 'talked out of it' by well-meaning outsiders. Encouragement from others may not be helpful to you during this stage of grieving, although at times the support of a strong shoulder and open ear might be appreciated.

As the shock of the loss fades, there is a tendency on the part of the griever to feel more pain and sadness. As a result, people who are grieving often feel more isolated or lonely as their grief progresses.

During this time, you finally realize the true magnitude of your loss and it depresses you. You may isolate yourself on purpose, reflect on things you did with your child and focus on memories of the past. You may sense feelings of emptiness or despair.

I felt somewhat lowly and self-centred to admit that I was desperately lonely when Danny died. It surprised me to read, years later, that loneliness is a common feeling for bereaved parents. We have lost someone we loved deeply and the greater the love, the greater the loneliness we feel.

People who are grieving are likely to fluctuate between wanting some time to themselves and wanting closeness with others, but when we isolate ourselves with no one to talk to about our feelings, we become depressed. Isolation plus depression is not a good thing.

Grief can make us feel very isolated. At times we may feel out of place and uncomfortable in company but sharing your feelings with other people can reduce the sense of isolation and loneliness that comes with grief. Allow people to help you. Don't be embarrassed to accept their help. You will be able to help someone else at another time. It is your turn now. Talk to family and friends or join a support group to share memories and stories, thoughts and feelings. This can be comforting and strengthen your connection with your loved one.

Most bereaved parents suffer a degree of depression at some time, but it is helpful to remember it is not a permanent state. The depression will pass when its purpose has been achieved, for most people. Gradually, you realise you have more energy to cope and will start to create a different sort of life. You will slowly find a new balance between moments of despair and moments of joy. These moments will eventually stretch out to longer periods of time.

You feel so alone when your child has died – so singled out by adverse fate in a world of happy and intact families. But we are really not alone. There are a lot more people suffering the same as you and me. In reality, I don't think it is true loneliness – more a feeling that you have been abandoned, let down, done unfairly, by life, by G-d. The presence and support of others in the same boat offer a degree of comfort.

After the week of *Shiva*, I experienced intense loneliness. My husband, following Danny's influence of doing as much Jewish observance as possible, went to *shule* for *Kaddish*, the mourner's prayer, three times a day for a year, even though the law requires just one month (unless it is for the death of a parent). My husband was an emotional wreck for that whole period – which thankfully, he cannot really remember.

My daughter, Renee, seven months pregnant when Danny died – soon had a newborn baby to deal with – '*Mazeltov, mazeltov!*'

And me – I was surrounded by people either consoling me on a death or congratulating me on a birth. I was bombarded and confused – and never felt so lonely in my life.

I was not the only one confused. I bumped into a friend of a friend several months later. 'Mazeltov,' she beamed, 'I hear Danny and Shelley had another baby. You must be so happy.' Agony.

Depression may include loss of appetite, sleeplessness, recurring bouts of sadness, lack of energy, lack of interest in what is going on around you and little reason to go on living. With the support of family and friends, many people adapt to loss over time. However, for some the experience of grief can be overwhelming and further support may be helpful.

Sometimes the circumstances of the death may have been particularly distressing, such as a traumatic or sudden death, or there may be circumstances in your life which make your grief particularly acute or complicated. If you are finding it difficult to manage on a day-to-day basis, it may be helpful to see a counsellor or other health professional. It is okay to admit you are struggling with your grief. No-one will think any less of you if you ask for help along the way

Will you ever get over it? The answer is yes – and no.

No – you will never be the same person. But yes, you do reach a point when remembering does not overpower you as it did in the beginning. You survive to see the day when you can love and laugh and enjoy the sunshine without feeling you are betraying your child by doing so.

Now, I am a more relaxed person. I am more observant of nature and see the beauty all around us. Often when I go for a walk with a friend I will point out the strange shape of a tree, unusual cloud formations or some other odd natural wonder. I was never aware of these displays of beauty before.

Research suggests that regular exercise may alleviate symptoms of depression by increasing energy levels, improving sleep, distracting us from worries, providing social support and reducing loneliness if done with other people. Allowing one to take an active role in one's own wellbeing increases a sense of control and self-esteem.

Reconstruction and working through

As your mind starts working again you will find yourself seeking realistic solutions to problems posed by life without your beloved child. You will start reconstructing yourself and your new life.

Just as you never get over being a parent, you will not 'get over' the death of your child. Instead, you will become 'reconciled' with it. In other words, you learn to live with it, despite being forever changed by it. But this does not mean a life of misery.

Through reconciliation, slowly the sharp pangs of grief will soften, and painful thoughts and feelings subside.

Rather than 'recovery' or 'resolution', which suggest a return to pre-loss functioning, 'reconciliation' and 'reconstruction' have been used to describe the post-death period because these terms more adequately reflect the profound changes that take place when a child dies.

In the book *The Worst Loss*[7], by Barbara D Rosof, the author states that it is only by allowing yourself to grieve that you can move toward a time and place where the grief does not consume you.

Many grieving parents emerge from the early years of grief as stronger, more capable people. They are more assertive and apt to say what they really believe. They do not concern themselves with trivialities. They have already suffered the worst life has to offer, so anything still to come cannot be so bad. They have learnt what is important and what's not. They may also discover (as I have) depths of compassion for others they did not know they had.

When Danny died it was as if our lives stopped. We were totally immobilised by our loss. If we don't grieve, for whatever reason – our lives remain stuck. The work of grief, of coming to terms with the realty that our child has died, is ultimately what enabled us to move ahead with our life, however altered it may be.

Acceptance and hope

During this stage, you learn to accept and deal with the reality of your situation. Acceptance does not necessarily mean instant happiness. Given the pain and turmoil you

---

[7] Worst Loss: How Families Heal from the Death of a
Child, Paperback – October 15, 1995, by Barbara D. Rosof

have experienced you can never return to the carefree, untroubled person that existed before this tragedy, but you will find a way forward.

The refusal to accept what we feel is unacceptable, only prolongs our anger and guilt, and produces bitterness. It does not relieve the deep aching inside us. The mindset which brings acceptance is accompanied by a degree of calmness.

We have all come across the poem by an American theologian Reinhold Niebuhr, written in 1934:

G-d grant me the serenity to accept the things I cannot change,
the courage to change the things I can,
and the wisdom to know the difference.

With serenity, acceptance, courage and change, comes wisdom – the realisation that some things which were so important before are no longer as important. Acceptance allows us to learn and mature as we travel this new road.

You will start to look forward and actually plan things for the future. Eventually, you will be able to think about your beloved child without wrenching pain. You will once again anticipate some good times to come and even find joy again in the experience of living.

Gradually, slowly, all the pent-up feelings begin to brighten. Instead of focusing only on death you will start to recall happier times and better memories. Grief will eventually lighten, guilt will resolve itself into regret and you will be able to let go of asking the unanswerable 'Why?' In time, you will return to life in a new, revised version. You will not only survive, you will find a measure of strength you never knew you had.

Yes, as time passes, we do begin to accept the death of our children, even though it is still hard to understand why it happened, and why it happened to us. We had no choice in it. Accepting Danny's death does not mean we have forgotten him. Far from it. That concept is totally unimaginable. Danny will always be our son.

OTHER POSSIBLE EFFECTS OF GRIEF

For those who have turned straight to this section, let me reiterate that I am by no means an expert on dealing with grief. There are many books written by doctors, psychologists, psychiatrists and grief counsellors. I am simply a mother who watched over her son with cancer until he died.

I also point out again that Danny had cancer for ten years. Some of the reactions that you may be experiencing now for the first time, are those I endured since Danny's diagnosis, so they were not new to me when he died.

Many of the emotional symptoms the mind experiences, like shock, denial, anger and depression, have been discussed in the previous section. However, grief-stricken parents may experience a host of other reactions too.

You may not experience any of these symptoms or you may be inundated by them. Remember, every one of us is different. Our circumstances, our relationship with our child, family dynamics and upbringing are different and can affect our reactions.

Physical symptoms

There are about two dozen ways in which our bodies may be affected by grief.

Some of these symptoms are discussed further in this section. The list is extensive and may include: overwhelming tiredness and exhaustion, restlessness, feeling unable to sit still, nausea, aches and pains, headaches, backache, neck pain, rib and chest pain, anxiety attacks or palpitations, flare-ups of previous conditions, tightness in the chest, difficulty breathing, appetite changes or digestive issues, hypertension, finding it hard to sleep or fear of sleeping, getting sick more often and other ailments.

It may be necessary to consult a medical specialist if any of these symptoms are causing concern.

Mental health

I have read that mental health involves cognitive thinking and harnessing your attention to stay focused. After Danny died there were times when I felt like a part of my brain had been cut away – not just a part of my heart. My 'normal' planning for the future had been aborted.

Consequently, I don't project my thoughts as much as before. I tell myself that this may be age-related. Danny was diagnosed in 1999, survived for ten years and it is now more than a decade since he died. I am more than twenty years older than I was when we were advised of Danny's death sentence.

Initially, I felt a sense of failure because I could not protect our child. I acknowledge now that Danny's illness and ultimate death were out of my control, yet at times I still feel a bit out of whack. I know Danny is no longer with us, but in my heart and mind I go on searching for him. Sometimes I might think I hear his voice or see him in a crowd – another young man, short hair, maybe with the tassels of his *tzitzit*[8] hanging out from his pants – for sure it's Danny!

I know that tears are an important way to express anguish. Allow yourself to cry when and where you need to. Recently, on the way back from a weekend shopping expedition, I burst out crying over Danny's death – the intense yearning, the sense of despair and disappointment was overwhelming. It can come at any time.

Since Danny's death my priorities have changed as have, I suppose, my personality and sense of humour.

I did see some counsellors throughout Danny's illness and was also in touch with over 350 other people with the same cancer, dozens of whom subsequently passed away. So, although never 'prepared' I knew I would outlive my son. I did think Danny would live at least another dozen or so years, but his death was not the blinding shock to me as it was to others. Sadly, the oncologist's prognosis was spot on.

But everyone's circumstances are different. You may require some temporary professional help as you regain control and stability in your life. Be careful of expecting too much too soon.

---

[8] *Tzitzit* – the fringes or tassels attached to a four-cornered garment worn by men, under the shirt.

Negative thoughts

As parents, we take on the role of protecting our children. Even when they grow up, leave home, get married and have children of their own, we still feel a sense of responsibility for them.

It is inevitable for many to feel a sense of in adequacy when their child dies.

'It's my fault, it should have been me, what did I do wrong?'

It is also usual for many parents to question themselves: 'Why me, how can I go on living, does this pain last forever, why go on?'

One of the main reasons I started the support group and why I feel so passionate about helping others who are in this same situation, is that when Danny died I was overcome with the emotion of 'why me'. I cried that I did not know any other Jewish families who had suffered in this way. I felt totally alone, alienated and desperate.

Then it was brought to my attention (I would have known it earlier but put it out of my mind) that the two families who lived opposite my house, in a small street made up of thirty homes, had both suffered the death of a child. In one of these houses, there is a weekly *shiur* (study session) in memory of three young girls from the same Jewish primary school, who all died in the one year.

I was not alone, after all.

Emotional health

To a degree, our emotional health is tied in with our mental stability. It involves expressing and working through our emotions, which may help determine how we cope. This may prevent unnecessary and unhealthy stress and depression.

From my own experience, the first year was a blur. My daughter had a new baby. My husband went to *shule* three times a day – we both have almost no recollection of the whole first year. We were totally numb. We were devastated and inconsolable. We could not think straight – we could not think at all! By the second year, reality had set in and other feelings emerged.

Emotionally, we felt battered. Our egos and belief in ourselves were shattered because as parents, we truly believed we could protect our child from anything.

You may feel you are going crazy, feel totally alone, scared, even thinking you would be happier if you joined your beloved child. For ten years I lived with the excruciating, diabolical fear that Danny would deteriorate and suffer incapacitation and immense pain. Perhaps irrationally, I debated with myself if he and I would be better off leaving this earth prematurely.

(As I write, the Euthanasia Bill has recently been passed in Victoria. I don't think I could stand by passively and watch my son, with an incurable, terminal disease, if he was in never-ending agony.)

Certainly, at times I feel confused, lonely, hypersensitive to others' comments, misunderstood, less secure within myself and resentful.

Particularly around the month of September I think of escaping or running away from the crushing barrage of emotions that bombard me. Danny was born on 6 September 1979. He died on 22 September 2008, eight days before *Rosh Hashanah*. The first *Yahrzeit* was on what would have been Danny's thirtieth birthday. We commemorate his *Yahrzeit*, then a week later we praise

G-d and ask to be written in the Book of Life. That just doesn't work for me.

Resentment

It is hard not to feel resentment, especially in the early days. I remember being resentful of old people when Danny was diagnosed, aged nineteen. Watching eighty and ninety-year-olds hobbling across the street – it didn't seem fair. Although I am a much more compassionate person than before, I confess I still suffer a bit from that emotion at times.

Recently, a very good friend of mine hosted a big party to celebrate her seventieth birthday. I speak to this friend almost daily and she was a great source of support for me throughout Danny's illness, and ongoing. We met, together with lots of other mums, when our children started school. She maintained a relationship with many of these people while I drifted, although I kept up a brief acquaintance while our children were friends in primary school.

I didn't want to go to a party and make small talk with these past friends, to catch up and remember the 'good times'. None of them sent a condolence card or came to a *minyan* for Danny, even though he was in class with their children. I know from experience how they will carefully avoid mentioning Danny for fear of making me feel uncomfortable. They are the ones feeling the discomfort.

I have read that, unfair as it seems, it is up to the bereaved parent to bring up the subject – and without any hint of resentment – if you do want to rekindle such relationships.

Inability to concentrate

For the first couple of years my attention span was often exceedingly short. I read two pages of a book and lost interest. I stopped trying for a while. I read parts of the newspaper and could not remember a word. I wrote myself notes because otherwise I would not remember anything.

This is a common conflict between two instinctive inner drives. The first drive demands that the grieving person strives to make sense of the loss, while the second drive reacts to the horror of the death of the child and works to block it out.

When I look back there were times when I couldn't think, could not remember from one minute to the next. I was told to be patient, that given time and some effort I would return to normal. Subconsciously, I did not want to think too hard, so I avoided it.

I do lose things around the house, but unless it's my keys, phone or wallet, I don't worry about it anymore. I know I will eventually come across the Vegemite in the freezer, the milk in the pantry or the Glad Wrap in the fourth drawer down with the handtowels.

Lack of energy and motivation

Grief is very tiring. Following the death of your child you may feel drained most of the time. This may last for months, especially if the death was unexpected.

It will probably take all your willpower to cook dinner each night and the food will have little or no appeal to you. Good nutrition is especially important for grievers. You need every source possible to regain your strength. Try to eat well-balanced meals and avoid overindulging.

You may have little or no energy and find it difficult to be enthusiastic about any task or project. You might listlessly do what is required of you but experience no joy from completing any jobs. Social events you once relished may now seem dull.

Fatigue, loss of short-term memory and lack of concentration will all improve gradually. With increasing energy, the capacity to organize daily life will slowly re-emerge.

Some form of physical outlet is necessary for the release of emotional stimuli. This is because the anxiety and tension of grieving manifests in the muscular tissue. Take a walk, do yoga or find some other way to increase your heart rate. Depression will be minimised with even a ten-minute walk.

Susceptibility to illness

During this time our bodies may have an unusually low resistance to illness. It is important to look after yourself. Physical exhaustion is a very common symptom of early bereavement. It can be a mistake to waste energy on trying to be in control when you feel far from it. Be yourself whenever possible. Try to eat sensibly and rest as much as you can, even though sleep may elude you. Walks and exercise in the fresh air may help restore sleep patterns and other relaxation techniques may help you too.

Sleeplessness

Sleep habits may become erratic or disturbed. Unless absolutely necessary try to avoid sleeping pills, especially over long periods of time, because they can become addictive. If you are having difficulty sleeping, try natural aids instead of drugs. Drinking a glass of warm milk, listening to soothing music, reading quietly or praying are all good ways to relax as you prepare for sleep. Avoid getting overstimulated close to bedtime and choose your activities carefully.

The light of a computer, mobile phone or electronic tablet is enough to cue your brain and signal wakefulness in your body. By engaging in screen time at bedtime you disrupt your natural wake-sleep cycle. This disruption makes it harder for you to unwind and sleep peacefully at night and get the rejuvenating, quality sleep your body needs.

Maybe some images keep coming to mind, certainly some distressing thoughts – reliving of the last moments, or the moment you found out about your child's death. Danny was diagnosed four days after my mum died. My upbringing dictated that I should not listen to music for a year after a parent's death, but I had my CD player nearby, for when I found it hard to get to sleep or if I woke during the night. I stuck blu-tac on the play button so I could easily feel for it in the dark, ready to press and replay at any time.

There are many reasons for not sleeping, one of the main ones being the amount of adrenaline trapped in your body. Adrenaline is the stress hormone produced when we are in danger. Bereavement has been regarded as the most potent form of stress the body has to withstand, so we produce enormous amounts of adrenaline to help us.

Spiritual conflict

I think the death of a child is one of the most challenging attacks on a person's belief in G-d. For me, after praying fervently for ten years, knowing that Danny was praying and members of the community were praying, his death felt like a rejection from G-d.

I can rationalise it now. It was just bad luck Danny got cancer. These things happen. Life is unpredictable. Maybe I should be happy that G-d granted Danny ten extra years after diagnosis to get all the things done that were important to him, to complete his education, get married, to father a child. Or, Danny was 'chosen' and is in a better place. I certainly do feel Danny is in a better place, feels no pain and is somehow not aware of the impact of his leaving us.

I am definitely not happy that Danny died. I am not worried about how he is. However, I am angry, very angry, at G-d, regardless of what His reasons were, for allowing Danny to get the cancer which caused his death.

I find myself feeling less enthused about Judaism than previously. I feel that G-d didn't listen to me before, so I find it superfluous to pray to Him now.

Other influences

Each person's grief reactions are unique and multi-dimensional. They are influenced by our personality and upbringing, our previous life experiences and the support system available to us.

Suicide and substance abuse

I have been in touch with over fifty families in which a child has died and in nearly twenty percent the cause of death was suicide or overdose.

I am not in that situation personally, but well aware of the special emotional angst these parents feel. I know each of these parents cared so much about their child and no one could ever accuse them of being to blame. Yet many don't come to our support group for fear of being judged, although this is definitely not the case. I told a bereaved mum that my relationship is with her, one fellow bereaved mum to another – the cause of her daughter's death does not affect my consideration for her.

Those who lose a loved one from suicide or drug abuse are more at risk at becoming preoccupied with the reason for their child's desperation, while wanting to deny or hide the cause of death. They wonder if it could have been prevented and maybe feel blame for the problems that preceded it, or for missing the signs of their child's desperation, feeling somehow responsible for their child's death.

The most essential ingredient in surviving well, besides facing reality, is to speak of the dead child unashamedly.

One lady I know, if asked, will tell you her daughter died during the night. Another will say that her son died in the shower.

One member pointed out to me that often the way people describe such a death is that they 'commit' suicide, like you commit a crime. The correct term is that

Suicide used to be a crime, hence the word 'commit'. Thankfully, taking's one's own life stopped being a crime in Australia several decades ago, so we can stop using that cruel word. Today, the law recognises that tragic and complex factors may surround a person's decision. People experiencing suicidal thoughts need help and support, not accusation. We must all try not to refer to it in this manner.

WE GRIEVE DIFFERENTLY

Men's and women's grief

Every individual grieves differently. Many factors contribute to how we grieve, such as the circumstance of the death, the nature of your relationship with your child, any previous experience you have had with death or other hardships, the strength of your network and your current life circumstances.

In addition, men and women grieve differently, so it may be hard for husband and wife, both suffering over the death of their child, to give support to each other. It is important to understand and accept these differences and respect each other's feelings.

Bear in mind also, that many of us have chosen a partner whose personality is different from our own. Our personality influences how we deal with grief.

In addition, the symptoms of grief ebb and flow among the various members of the family and allowances must be made for this.

My husband was born in a German concentration camp and struggled to survive infancy. He saw his six-foot tall, dark and handsome son as a beacon for life and hope, and to some degree as a symbol of immortality on behalf of his ancestors.

Meanwhile, I sat through endless appointments with Danny's oncologists at Peter MacCallum Cancer Hospital, being told repeatedly that there was no change, no hope, no future, while his life was being maintained with unsustainable toxic treatments.

The timing, the circumstances, indeed the eventuality was not such a shock to me as it was to my husband.

Grieving partners may find it difficult to support each other well in the early weeks and months of their grief. They are simply too overcome with their own thoughts and feelings to be truly helpful to someone else. This is normal and not a marital failure.

Also, it may be hard to offer comfort and support to your partner when you are desperately in need of it yourself.

Mothers sometimes feel they are more affected by the death of a child and there is research to support that a mother's grief is often more disabling and longer-lasting. If the child was living at home the mother may be more aware, because day-to-day routines for her children are now different. The child is no longer included in the work of washing, shopping, cooking and buying clothes.

Women are typically more outwardly emotional and slower to return to daily routines. When we become mothers, our lives change. Our children become our highest priority and we accept new and wide responsibilities. We forgo sleep and divert our energy into meeting their needs ahead of our own. Mothers are often the main care-givers to their children, particularly at a younger age. We grow with our child as they grow, from total dependence to learning new skills. As our child grows the memories of the physical and emotional care we give are part of the bond between us.

Fathers feel the same depths of grief, but may tend to suppress these feelings, often appearing more stoical. Many men feel they are expected to be strong, to be in control of their emotions and tend to rush back to work faster. Sometimes the workplace may be a retreat from the pressures of home.

It may be hard for some people to understand, but for some men having a son fulfils a filial obligation to the paternal grandparents to carry on the family name. The death of an only son seems to obliterate family heritage.

Below is a table compiled by Katrin Ringehahn.[9] While this is a good overview it is a gender-based generalisation, in the 'Men are from Mars, Women are from Venus' style.

Grieving mothers very often ...	Grieving fathers very often ...
need to talk	don't want to talk
cry a lot and seek out support groups	hide their pain and make it on their own
ask the same questions again and again, hoping to find understanding	don't know what else to answer, wishing they could fix things
read books on grief and write to sort out the pain	disappear into the shed not to be seen again
feel he should grieve her way	need space to grieve their way

[9] Ringehahn, Katrin, on her website http://www.positive-parenting-skills.net. Permission to include obtained by Katrin Ringehahn

seek understanding and hugs to feel close	look for closeness in sexual intimacy
need 9 - 24 months or more to resolve their grief	make peace with their grief in 3-6 months
have the impression their partners don't grieve	feel their spouses needs professional help after 6 months

Intuitive and instrumental grief

In recent years research has produced new theories and models about the way we grieve, which show a less gender-based interpretation.

No model is going to be an exact fit for an individual. But what is certain is that we do respond to grief across many dimensions: with emotions, with our thoughts, with our behaviour, with our physical reactions and we can be affected spiritually as well.

There is talk of new grieving styles: the 'Intuitive' style versus the 'Instrumental' style. Researcher Kenneth Doka[10] is credited with much of the work in this field.

Doka observed that with people who are highly intuitive find it helpful to find some place, whether in therapy, with a confidante, in a support group, or in their own journaling or internal process, to explore their feelings. These feelings are characterized by extreme sadness and pain as well as an outward experience characterized by emotional expression. They find comfort in talking about

---

[10] Grieving Beyond Gender by Kenneth J Doka, published by Taylor and Francis Group LLC, 2010. Permission obtained from the author

their loved one as often as possible and may find it hard to think about the future, preferring to dwell on the past and the present.

On the other hand, instrumental grievers respond to their grief in more physical or cognitive ways, thinking for an answer or focusing on the future. Instrumental grievers prefer to grieve alone and try to think their way out of their grief. Their outward experience is characterized by lack of emotion, while none-the-less being productive or active in their grief, like doing research or setting up some memorial in honour of their child.

Men and women do tend to deal with their grief differently. A generalisation about gender differences would describe men as spending more time thinking than feeling. They also prefer to sort out their problems on their own. They would rather do something about their loss than talk about it – Instrumental Grievers. Women typically are more expressive about their emotions, seek support and speak more openly about their feelings – Intuitive Grievers.

But when all things are considered, people shouldn't feel bad about not fitting neatly into a category – our grief is our own and we no doubt do the best we can with what we can handle at the time.

Blended grieving - It is also noted that intuitive and instrumental grieving are two extreme styles of grieving located on a scale. Because of this, it is rare to find people who belong purely to one style of a grieving pattern. The middle area between extreme intuitive grieving and extreme instrumental grieving is called blended grieving. People who exhibit qualities of both the intuitive grieving style as well as the instrumental grieving style are identified as blended grievers. Through blended grieving, a person naturally expresses grief in both cognitive (from the head, instrumental) and affective (from the heart, intuitive) ways, however one style of grief is usually more dominant than the other.

In addition, one's own responses may change. It was pointed out to me by a grief counsellor reviewing the draft of this book, that while most of my emotions are intuitive, after many years of seeking solace, I am now pro-actively reaching out to others.

Again, it is vital that partners recognise, understand and tolerate each other's needs and can support each other. There may be times when one parent wants to talk about the death and be emotive and the other one wants to fix it somehow. At some point when they realise they can't fix it, they may start to withdraw, and that is when fractures in a relationship can start to happen.

A descriptions of Intuitive and Instrumental grievers [11]can be shown thus:

Intuitive grievers …		Instrumental grievers …
Openly express emotions	←Blending→	Push aside feelings to cope with the present
Allow time to experience inner pain		Choose active or physical ways of expressing grief
Can discuss the grief		Use humour or anger to express feelings
Identify others as sources of support		Seeks solitude to reflect and adapt to loss
Choose ways to express feelings – journals, craft		Wants to only be around close friends/confidants
May benefit from support groups		May not do well in a support group

[11] Complied by Australian Centre for Grief and Bereavement

Children's grief

My daughter, Renée, was already an adult when Danny died, so I have no personal experience of the effect of a death on a young sibling.

Below is a summary of what I have learnt.

Do not underestimate the grief of your other children. Children cannot sustain emotional pain in the way adults can, so they tend to move in and out of grief, crying initially and later remaining dry-eyed, even when adults around them are crying.

Visually, the comparison between an expressive adult's grief and that of a child or adolescent may appear dramatically different, making it easy for adults to make sweeping pronouncements such as, 'Children are resilient and get over things easily; they soon forget'. Remarks like this are inaccurate and often make bereaved children and young people angry. They feel as if their grief is minimised at best and believed non-existent at worst.

Let the children see your emotions. If you repress them they are more likely to repress their own. They must feel they can show grief openly and mourn without fear or embarrassment.

Children and young people frequently cry on the inside. Tears outwardly expressed make them feel embarrassed, different and vulnerable. They desperately need to remain part of the group, no different to their peers. They need to convince themselves that life will continue in a positive way, despite their experience of loss.

Children of different ages react differently – and I am not the right person to discuss this. Please seek help from a professional experienced with bereaved siblings if you feel this will help your children. It is vital that grieving siblings do not become the forgotten mourners. They need to know that their grief is important too.

Be aware of the change in family dynamics that your child or children are experiencing. If you had two children before, your surviving child is now an only child. At twenty years old, my daughter was amazed at how much she missed her brother, Danny, when he went overseas during his gap year after Year Twelve. Now she is forever an only child.

A heavy sense of responsibility is another common childhood grief reaction. If a sibling has died, the remaining child or children may feel they have to be of such value to their parents that they fill the void, make the parents happy again and give them a reason for living.

Our grief may prompt us to overprotect our other children. Some siblings may fear getting sick, if they lost a brother or sister because of illness. Give plenty of reassurance and affection. Let them know you love them and are there for them. Take time to listen to them. Let them know their feelings are important.

When we, as adults, grieve the same death our children grieve it is often difficult to find the energy, patience and creativity required to provide the help our surviving children need.

Your home should still be a sanctuary for them and you must not forget their needs. Kids need time, understanding, space and re-assurance. They need to be held and listened to. Be sure to rejoice in their achievements.

<u>WHERE IS G-D IN ALL THIS?</u>

One day, a son asked his father, 'Why is it always the best people who die?'
The father answered, 'Son, if you are in a meadow, which flowers do you pick?
The worst ones or the best?'   **Author unknown**

Religion may have either a positive or negative impact on how we grieve, but some evidence suggests that parents with strong religious faith fare better in grieving than others.

If we recognize our need to talk about our loss, we might think of prayer as a personal conversation with G-d in which, by recounting our story and that of our child, we seek healing. I do envy those with this strength of faith.

You may be angry with G-d and question how a loving and omnipotent G-d could deprive you of your child. This attitude is understandable and apparently remains the primary attitude for a large percentage of bereaved parents turning away from religion rather than to it.

Negative thoughts following a child's death may cast doubt on the existence of G-d and loss of faith may continue for many years – or forever. Even if you believe in an afterlife, you have still lost precious time together with your child on earth.

I certainly do not understand how survivors of the Holocaust kept their faith.

In the book of *Kohelet* (Ecclesiastes), it says:

To everything there is a season
And a time to every purpose under heaven
A time to be born, and a time to die.

I believe G-d knew when Danny was going to die. I believe G-d planned it. Maybe on the day Danny was born. Yes, I surely believe G-d exists, but I readily admit I'm not happy with Him.

There is a story of someone who prayed to G-d to save his son, and his son died. When questioned if he still believed in G-d, he said 'Of course'. 'But how can you', he was asked, 'when G-d did not answer your prayers'. 'Yes, he did', replied the man, 'but this time his answer was 'No'.

The fact that you are reading this book, shows your continued affinity with Judaism. In our support group there are some who are observant, some who married out, some who brought their children up with no religion at all, others who made quite different choices – yet they still feel a need to come back to their roots in their time of despair.

A RICH TAPESTRY – OR A BUNDLE OF KNOTS?

No farewell words were spoken, no time to say goodbye. You were gone before we knew it, and only G-d knows why. **Author unknown**

For ten years people around the world prayed for Danny. Every *Shabbat*, as I lit my candles, I begged G-d to look after Danny. Some might say G-d did answer and He gave Danny those ten extra years. I know that Danny is in a better place. I have absolutely no doubt at all about that.

But I miss him. I want him here, with me, with his wife, watching over his growing child, fulfilling the dreams he planned for his future here on earth.

When Danny died a very observant fellow bereaved mother tried to console me with the tale that life was a tapestry, looking beautiful to us observers, but we never think to look at the back – to see the stops and starts of our being, to see that this 'life' we are having now is just a segment of our being. We don't know G-d's plan. Like a tapestry, we only see the front, not understanding all that has happened until this point. The life we are living now is part of not just this century, or last century, or 6,000 years, but part of eternity.

When people talk of miracles, I cringe! Miracles don't exist in real life. But, then again, maybe they do. Danny survived ten years riddled with over one hundred tumours.

AN OVERVIEW OF JEWISH LAWS AND CUSTOMS

I believe in the sun, even when it isn't shining.
I believe in love, even when there's no one there.
And I believe in G-d, even when he is silent.

- written during WW2, on the wall of a cellar, by a Jewish prisoner in a Cologne concentration camp.

The following is provided as an outline. If you want additional information refer to the Chevra Kadisha or your own burial society, any rabbi or the internet. There are also several books in the JBP library which might assist.

Judaism is not just a religion but a state of the heart and of the soul. Each family must determine its own level of observance and adherence to traditional practices. This book is not intended to differentiate between any level of observance and attitudes and is merely an overview of proceedings.

In Australia there are essentially three branches of Judaism: Orthodox, Progressive and Conservative. There are also those who decry Judaism completely – yet when their child dies, they often feel the need to re-affirm their Jewish roots.

SHEMIRA

Shemira refers to watching over the body until burial. It is a custom practiced out of respect for the dead. They should not be abandoned prior to their arrival in their new 'home' in the ground. This serves as a comfort for the surviving loved ones as well.

According to tradition, the soul hovers over the body for up to seven days after death feeling somewhat lost and confused, and it stays in the general vicinity until the body is buried. Traditionally the *shomrim* (or guard/s) sit and read aloud comforting psalms during the time they are watching the body. This serves as a comfort for both the spirit of the departed, who is in transition, and the *shomer* or *shomeret*[12] who are prohibited from eating,

---

[12] *Shomer* – a male guard watching over the deceased male before burial,
Shomeret – a female guard watching over the deceased female
Shomrim – the plural term for guards

drinking, or smoking in the *shemira*[13] room out of respect for the dead who can no longer do these things.

A group of Danny's friends watched over his body throughout the night. I am certain this was not something they ever expected to do, and probably something they will never forget. My gratitude to these boys is unending.

K'RIAH

The rending of mourner's clothing, *k'riah*, on hearing the news of their loss, symbolises the tearing of their heart. Over time, this has become formalised into cutting an outer garment, or even pinning on and cutting a piece of ribbon. When one is mourning for parents *k'riah* is performed on the left side, over the heart. When mourning for children, siblings and spouses, it is done on the right side.

FUNERAL

The funeral of your child is likely to be one of the worst days of your life. Possibly the reason you don't collapse completely is because you are numb with disbelief. I imagine it has taken place by the time you are reading this, so I will simply refer you to a few sites that can provide further details if required:

---

[13] *Shomera* – the room where the guard/s sit and watch over the deceased.

Orthodox: Melbourne Chevra Kadisha – mck.org.au, 03 9534 0208
Progressive: Beit Olam – jewishfunerals.org.au, 03 9883 6237
Conservative: Kehilat Nitzan – kehilatnitzan.org.au 03 9500 0906

These sites are in Melbourne. Please search for similar sites in your state.

KADDISH

Kaddish is a hymn in which, despite our loss, we still praise G-d. It is the most recognized prayer in the Jewish liturgy. It was composed in Aramaic, the language of the *Talmud*. Some sources[14] say that *Kaddish* originated not in the synagogue but in the house of study. After a scholar delivered a learned discourse, students and teachers rose to praise G-d's name. During the mourning period for a rabbi or teacher, students gathered to study in his honour, and his son was given the honour of leading the prayer. Over time, reciting *Kaddish* replaced studying as the tribute given to a scholar. Eventually, the custom extended to all mourners, not only the survivors of rabbis and leaders. By the sixth century, *Kaddish* was part of synagogue prayers. During the thirteenth century, when the Crusades threatened Jewish communities in Europe, it became inextricably linked to loss and mourning.

Kaddish is not a prayer on behalf of the deceased. It is the prayer of sanctification of G-d's name. In Jewish tradition names are regarded as more than just labels. Names reflect the nature and identity of what they refer to, so the

---

[14] www.myjewishlearning.com

prayer that G-d's name be exalted is like glorifying G-d Himself.

It is extremely difficult for someone absolutely devastated by the loss of his loved one, to come to the realization that everything that G-d does is for the good. People in this situation tend to question their faith and question the meaning of life. This is why the rabbis required mourners to strengthen their faith, by reciting *Kaddish* as an affirmation of their trust and belief in G-d.

There are several forms of *Kaddish*, each said at various times.

For a child, *Kaddish* is said for thirty days after burial, although some people choose to say it for longer.

Most Orthodox *shules* do not permit a woman to say *Kaddish*, but attitudes are changing and some are broadening their attitudes towards women participants. Progressive and Conservative synagogues permit women to be part of the service.

In addition to the standard order of prayers, some additional text is also recited, often lines from the *Mishnah*[15] corresponding with the initial letters of the name of the deceased.

SHIVA

There are three recognised steps of mourning before ultimately returning to the 'new normality', without our

---

[15] *Mishnah* – the Oral law, as opposed to the written Torah. The Mishnah was collected and committed to writing around the year 200 and forms part of the Talmud.

---

loved one. There is the first week (*Shiva*), the first month (*Shloshim*) and the first year (consecration and first *Yahrzeit*).

Shiva is a Hebrew word meaning 'seven'. It refers to the seven-day period of formalized mourning. Jewish law dictates that mourners need not wallow alone in their grief; on the contrary, it is important to share grief with others and surround oneself with friends, family and fellow mourners. The mourners customarily do not leave the 'Shiva house' through the entire week, and friends and acquaintances visit there. It is commendable to focus conversations on the merits of the deceased.

Shiva begins immediately after the funeral, when we gather together at home and cut ourselves off from the normal routine of our lives.

The psychological wisdom of seven days of intense grief has been recognised by virtually every bereavement expert.

The candle

A candle will be provided by the burial society. This is lit when the mourners arrive home from the cemetery and will last for the seven days of *Shiva*. The candlelight is the symbol of the human being. The wick and the flame symbolise body and soul and the bond between them. The flame in the soul that strives forever upwards and brings light into darkness [16]

---

[16] Refer to the website chabad.org

The meal of condolence

The first meal upon returning from the cemetery is called the *Seudat Havraah*, literally 'the meal of recuperation'. This is usually provided by family and friends and typically includes foods that are round, like hard boiled eggs and bagels, to symbolise the cycle of life.[17]

Low chairs

Mourners sit on low chairs to symbolise their awareness that life is not the same and that they want to be close to the earth in which their loved one is buried.

Mirrors

While in mourning it is not appropriate to be concerned with personal vanity, so mirrors should be covered[18]. I was brought up to believe that you also cover glassed pictures on the walls, so as not to see your reflection in them, but I can't find any reference to this.

Other customs

Jewish tradition prohibits certain activities for the mourner during *Shiva*. Throughout the week of *Shiva* mourners do not work. Friends and neighbours may take responsibility for preparing your food, serving it to you,

---

[17] Refer to the website jewish-funeral-guide.com

[18]

www.jewishmag.com/140mag/mirror_mourning/mirror_mourning.htm

cleaning up and doing whatever they can to make the days easier for you.

During this week, tradition discourages bathing for pleasure, changing or laundering clothing, cutting hair or shaving, applying makeup or cream, wearing leather shoes, cutting nails, engaging in marital relations and participating in joyous events. These practices are based upon minimising the mourner's joy, but they are not observed on *Shabbat.*

Different people regard these customs with varying levels of strictness.

Tradition also suggests that shaking hands, hugging or kissing mourners is discouraged and that guests do not initiate conversation with the mourner, but wait for the mourner to start talking to them. Upon leaving the mourner's house it is customary to say,

Hamö-kom y'na-chaym es-chem   הַמָּקוֹם יְנַחֵם אֶתְכֶם

b'soch sh'ör avay-lay   בְּתוֹךְ שְׁאָר אֲבֵלֵי

tzi-yon viru-shölö-yim.   צִיּוֹן וִירוּשָׁלָיִם :

Translation:
May the Almighty comfort you among the mourners of Zion and Jerusalem.

LONG LIFE

I was so angry throughout the week of *shiva.* I did not understand the true meaning of being wished a 'long life' when my son had just died. How can I enjoy a long life when I am wracked in misery?

However, Rabbi Aron Moss from Nefesh Shul in Sydney explained it thus: 'In the original Hebrew, the blessing is, "May you have long days." Some of us are blessed with long lives, some not. But we can all have long days[19].

'A long day is a day full of meaning, a day spent doing good, spreading happiness and fulfilling a purpose. A day of giving and loving, learning and teaching, building spirits and lifting souls – that is a long day.

'Some achieve in a short lifetime what others never get around to doing. The difference is not how you spend your life, but how you spend your day. We don't choose how many days we live, but we can choose how we live our days. The length of our days is not measured in hours on the clock, but in beats of the heart, not in minutes, but in *mitzvahs.*

'When we suffer the loss of a loved one, we become more sharply aware of how precious just one day can be. A wasted day is an eternity lost. And a day well spent can have an eternal impact.

'Yes, there's always tomorrow, but there's only one today. And we have many lifetimes, but this one we only live once. Don't wait for tomorrow. Time is short, make today a long day.'

I have also come across another explanation about 'long life' which said that when one is grieving one cannot feel any happiness or joy and that the thoughts of your loved one bring only sadness and grief. Therefore, one wishes someone will have a 'long life' so that over time, the person grieving can again participate in life and have good memories of the deceased.

---

[19] www.israelnationalnews.com/Articles/Article.aspx/6760

SHLOSHIM

Shloshim is the Hebrew word for 'thirty'. This extended period of mourning concludes on the morning of the thirtieth day. Even as the mourner resumes his or her everyday routine after sitting *Shiva*, certain mourning practices, such as not purchasing or wearing new clothes, cutting one's hair, enjoying music or other forms of entertainment, and participating in joyous events are continued for a period of thirty days. These restrictions are designed to protect the bereaved from finding themselves in situations that are very difficult to bear psychologically.

At the end of *Shloshim*, the deceased's family visits the grave. Some people erect a tombstone at this point while others wait until the first anniversary of the death. At the grave, it is customary to recite verses from Psalms, the mourner's *Kaddish* (assuming there is a *minyan*), and *Maleh Rachamim*[20], a prayer for the soul of the person who has died.

CEMETERY VISITS

After the funeral you should not visit the cemetery until after the *Shiva* period, then again after *Shloshim* and on the anniversary of your child's death.

Thereafter, many people visit the cemetery preceding a *Yomtov*, particularly *Rosh Hashanah* and *Yom Kippur*,

---

[20]

https://www.chabad.org/library/article_cdo/aid/367837/jewish/
Kel-Maleh-Rachamim.htm

because these are reflective days, when one is truly focused on what is really important in life. We pray to *G-d* and ask our loved one to be an advocate to Him on our behalf.

While visiting the grave at any other time is permitted, excessive visits are discouraged. We mourn, but we must set boundaries to our mourning. To not mourn at all, or to plunge into an abyss of grief, is damaging both to the living and to the soul of the departed. Mourning is a show of respect to the departed and to his or her place in our lives, as well as a crucial stage in the healing of those who experienced the loss. The soul of the departed does not desire that those remaining in this world remain paralysed by grief. On the contrary, the soul's greatest benefit comes from its loved ones' return to active, even joyous life, in which their feelings of love and respect translate into deeds that honour the departed soul and attest to its continuing influence in our world.[21]

LEAVING A STONE

The Hebrew word for pebble is *tz'ror*, which means bond. When we pray at the gravesite we ask that the deceased be 'bound up in the bond of life' (*tz'ror hahayyim*). Unlike flowers, a stone will never die, symbolising the permanence of memory and legacy.

The tradition of leaving a pebble on top of the tombstone probably comes from the ancient practice of sealing the grave with a large gravestone to mark the grave and

---

[21] https://www.chabad.org/library/article_cdo/aid/282506/jewish/The-Stages-of-Mourning-in-Judaism.htm

prevent scavengers from disturbing it. Nowadays it shows that we have been there and that the individual's memory continues to live on, in and through us. The pebble should be placed using the left hand.

A very early reference to this custom is found in a commentary to the *Shulchan Aruch*[22], which explains that the custom of placing stones or tufts of grass on the grave is for the honour of the deceased person by marking the fact that his grave has been visited.[23]

I follow my husband's tradition of placing some grass with a stone. I don't know anyone else who does this.

PLANNING THE TOMBSTONE

The tombstone (called a *matzevah* in Hebrew) can be erected any time after the *Shiva* period is over, although most people tend to wait longer, within the first year.

When a premature death occurs (meaning a child or young adult), it is customary that a corner of the tombstone is chipped off, to show that this life was cut short.

Usually one puts the two Hebrew letters at the top of the stone, פ *'pay'* and נ *'nun'*. This stands for *'po nikbar'*, meaning, 'Here is buried'.

(here insert list

---

[22] *Shulchan Aruch* – the Code of Jewish law, the most widely consulted text on legal codes in Judaism, first published in 1565

[23] https://ohr.edu/ask/ask222.htm

One also puts the following five letters below the rest of the inscription, written in Hebrew as: תנצבה (tav, nun, tzadik, bet hay)

ת *'tav'*, נ *'nun'*, צ *'tzadek'*, ב *'bet'* and ה *'hay'* – which stands for, 'May his/her soul be bound up in the bond of eternal life.'

It is also a good idea to go to the cemetery and see other stones.

CONSECRATION – THE UNVEILING

Although a common practice, a formal unveiling is not compulsory, but some form of tombstone is the norm. The erection of the tombstone is a tribute to the memory of the deceased and honours the body that housed the soul. For those whose family and friends who travelled from overseas for the burial, it may be preferable to erect the tombstone while they are still here.

The lead-up to the consecration is usually filled with anxiety. Unlike the burial which is sudden and immediately after the death, we put a lot of effort into planning the consecration. Weeks or months are spent designing the headstone and the anxiety builds as the date approaches. We are more aware than we were at the time of death. We are no longer in the same state of shock as at the funeral, and we have time to get anxious and torment ourselves with distress.

It is horrendous, seeing a tombstone with your child's name on it. But let's face it, these past weeks and months since your child died have been the worst of our lives. The service will pass. Try not to get too stressed in anticipation of it.

YAHRZEIT

Yahrzeit is a Yiddish word meaning anniversary of a death, traditionally the anniversary of the Hebrew date, not the Gregorian date. *Yahrzeit* is observed at home by lighting a special candle which burns for twenty-five hours. There is no specific blessing said when lighting the candle.

It is customary to visit the gravesite at this time and to give charity to mark the occasion.

In *shule*, *Yahrzeit* is observed by reciting the mourner's *Kaddish*.

YIZKOR

Yizkor means 'memorial' and is recited four times a year in *shule*: *Yom Kippur, Shemini Atzeret* (the last day of *Sukkot*), the eighth day of *Pesach* and the second day of *Shavuot*.

Originally *Yizkor* was only said on *Yom Kippur*[24]. Its primary purpose was to remember the deceased by giving *tzedakah* (a moral obligation to give charity to those in need), on the theory that good deeds of the survivors elevate the souls of the departed. Some say that since the *Torah* reading on the last day of the three festivals mentions the importance of donations, *Yizkor* was added to these holiday services.

---

[24] www.myjewishlearning.com

Some people have the custom of waiting a year before reciting *Yizkor* on behalf of their loved one.

Kaddish is not recited as part of *Yizkor* so there is no technical requirement for a *minyan*. Therefore, the memorial paragraphs can be said privately if you cannot attend *shule*.

I was shown this following prayer provided by LaJean Sturman and published by The Compassionate Friends in Texas. I do not know when it was printed and assume the contributor was Conservative or Progressive. She stated that at the beginning of the Jewish New Year there is a special service held in remembrance of loved ones and this prayer is for our children:

I remember in this solemn hour, beloved child, the many joys you afforded me during your lifetime. I recall the days when I delighted in your physical and mental growth and planned for your future. Though death has taken you from me, you are not forgotten. Your spirit is enshrined in my heart. Oh Lord, I thank thee for the precious gift which though did entrust to my keeping and which in Thine infinite wisdom Thou has called back unto Thyself. Though few were the years in which I rejoiced with my child, many are the blessings that my child brought into my household. Teach me to live more nobly and to extend my love and devotion to other children in thankfulness for the privilege of having had and loved this child, though but for a few brief years. Thus, may his (her) soul be bound up in the bond of life and his (her) memory remain an inspiration to me. Amen.

PRAYERS AT THE GRAVESITE

The main purpose of cemetery visits is to honour the deceased and to pray for the elevation of his or her soul. It is forbidden to pray to the dead or to ask anything from them (Deuteronomy 18:11) as if they can intercede on your behalf because they are closer to G-d.

The most significant prayer said at the gravesite is *Maleh Rachamim*, (literally G-d of mercy), a prayer of comfort about the soul ascending to the Garden of Eden. The primary benefit for the soul of the deceased is not just the memorial prayer, but the commitment to fulfil the charity pledges made in this prayer in their memory, to spiritually elevate their souls.

See footnote for a link to the words in Hebrew, transliteration or English.[25]

For more Orthodox Jews there are several specific psalms that can be recited. Some also recite the verses from Psalm 119 that begin with the letters of the name of the deceased, as well as those verses whose initial letters spell the word *neshamah* (Hebrew for 'the soul'). See footnote for additional prayers and explanations. [26]

REINCARNATION

I am definitely not an expert in this subject. The following is my simply an attempt to give a brief overview.

---

[25]

https://www.chabad.org/library/article_cdo/aid/367837/jewish/Kel-Maleh-Rachamim.htm

[26] http://www.jewish-funeral-guide.com/tradition/funeral-customs.htm

In his book the *Jewish Way in Death and Mourning*, Maurice Lamm wrote on the front cover 'Death is a night between two days'. Think about it – I never did before!

The notion that the soul will live on and that resurrection awaits is a cornerstone belief in Judaism. [27]

Each individual soul is dispatched to the physical world with its own individualized mission to accomplish. As Jews, we all have the same *Torah* with the same 613 *mitzvot* (commandments, good deeds). Each of us also has his or her own set of challenges, distinct talents and capabilities and particular *mitzvot* which form the core of his or her mission in life.

At times, a soul may not conclude its mission in a single lifetime. In such cases, it returns to earth for a 'second go' to complete the job. This is the concept of *Gilgul Neshamot* – commonly referred to as 'reincarnation' and extensively discussed in the teachings of *Kabbalah*[28]. This is the reason it is said that often we find ourselves powerfully drawn to a particular *mitzvah* or cause and make it the focus of our lives, dedicating to it a seemingly disproportionate part of our time and energy. It is our soul gravitating to the 'missing pieces' of its divinely ordained purpose. [29]

Body and soul will be reunited as they were before they were separated by death. The soul, for its part, remains involved in the lives of those it leaves behind when it departs physical life. Because the soul is no longer constricted by the limitations of

---

[27] Simon Shimshon Rubin, University of Haifa, Israel, Loss and Mourning in the Jewish Tradition, Baywood Publishing Co., Inc 2014

[28] *Kabbalah* – Often referred to as the 'soul' of the Torah, the *Kabbalah* is an ancient Jewish tradition which teaches the deepest insights into the essence of G-d, His interaction with the world, and the purpose of Creation

[29]

https://www.chabad.org/library/article_cdo/aid/303987/jewish/What-Happens-After-We-Die.htm the physical state, its relationship with its loved ones is, in many ways, even deeper and more meaningful than before.

However, while the departed soul is aware and cognizant of all that transpires in the lives of its loved ones, souls remaining in the physical world are limited to what they can perceive via the five senses, as facilitated by their physical bodies.

We can impact the soul of a departed loved one through our positive actions, but we cannot communicate with it through the conventional means (speech, sight, physical contact, etc.) that, prior to its passing defined the way we related to each other. (Indeed, the *Torah* expressly forbids the idolatrous practices of necromancy[30], seances and similar attempts to 'make contact' with the world of the dead.) Hence, the occurrence of death, while signifying an elevation for the soul of the departed, is experienced as a tragic loss for those it leaves behind.

Many people believe that ultimately, they will be reunited with their son or daughter, others without such a belief must accept that what they had with their child is all that will ever be, except for their memories. One lady in our group told me she envies me for my belief. I feel very sorry that although being optimistic on earth she feels she has nothing to look forward to in the afterlife.

BELIEF IN *OLAM HABA* – THE WORLD TO COME

I am definitely not an expert in this subject either. The following is my simply an attempt to give a brief overview.

One of the fundamental beliefs in Judaism is that life does not begin with birth, nor does it end with death. This is expressed

---

[30] Necromancy is the supposed practice of communicating with the dead, especially in order to predict the future

in the line in *Kohelet* (Ecclesiastes) 12:7 – "And the dust returns to the earth as it was, and the spirit returns to G-d, who gave it."

In these and numerous other communications, the Lubavitch Rebbe echoes the words of the great twelfth-century Jewish philosopher, Maimonides: 'Just as the blind cannot see the spectrum of colours and the deaf cannot hear sound, so too, the mortal body cannot understand the spiritual joys (attained in the Hereafter), which are eternal. These joys have nothing in common with the happiness derived from material things.'

Once humanity has completed its mission of making the physical world a 'dwelling-place for G-d,' comes the era of universal reward – the '*Olam HaBa*' (the world to come).[31]

In today's imperfect world the soul can experience 'reward' only after it departs from the body and physical life. In the world to come the soul and body will be reunited and will together enjoy the fruits of their labour. Thus, the prophets of Israel spoke of a time when all who died will be restored to life; their bodies will be regenerated and their souls restored to their bodies. [32]

For so long as the soul is bound up with the body, the soul suffers from the physical limitations of the body, which necessarily constrain the soul and involve it in physical activities that are alien to its purely spiritual nature. In other words, the departure of the soul from the body is a great advantage and ascent for the soul.

Personally, I am very confused as to where I stand regarding my devotion to G-d. But, I have found comfort in the thought that although Danny's physical body has departed his soul goes on living.

---

[31] https://www.chabad.org/library/article_cdo/aid/282508/jewish/What-Happens-After-We-Die.htm

[32] Also from chabad.org

<u>**LEARNING TO COPE**</u>

Think of your child, then, not as dead, but as living; not as a flower that has withered, but as one that is transplanted, and touched by a Divine hand, is blooming in richer colours and sweeter shades than those of earth. **Richard Hooker**, British theologian

Mark Twain, when asked about the death of his daughter, aged twenty-four, responded 'that to attempt to communicate about such a loss would bankrupt the languages of the world.'

There are no words to describe our tragedy. Burying a child stands the world on its head. Things don't make sense after your child's death. Your sense of personal and global equilibrium is shattered.

You feel it now and it is true for the rest of your days – you will never get over the death of your child. But you will go on. You go on as a changed person. You will never be the same person you were before, but you do reach the point where remembering does not overwhelm you as it did in the beginning. You survive to see the day when you can love and laugh and enjoy the sunshine without feeling that you are betraying your child by doing so. We heal, but we remember, and living with the memory is part of the healing.

Take comfort in other bereaved parents. I mentioned it earlier and it is worth repeating here – they have something many of your friends do not possess. Sadly, they have experience. They are examples of parents who have learnt to cope or are in the process of learning.

If someone asks me how I am, it has taken me years to feel, and now to actually admit that I am feeling okay.

But I only just realised the reason I'm okay is because, while I live with a massive hole in my heart because of the death of Danny, other things that upset everybody else don't upset me, don't get me down.

I no longer fuss over the little things: the cup is chipped, I've scratched the tabletop or my hair has gone frizzy. I no longer sweat the small stuff! My computer got hijacked and I didn't freak out. My priorities have changed.

To a very minor degree, it's like you lose an arm – you won't get over that, but you will learn to dress with one hand.

I am by nature quite stoical, probably due to my English parentage. But I find now I am stronger, yet a lot more emotional.

Psychologists may tell you they know how you feel, because in their minds your loss ranks equally with the loss of a spouse or parent or with losing your job or your house burning down. But I feel they are wrong.

Both my parents died before Danny. I had been retrenched a few times. I left the toaster on one night and burned down the kitchen and we had a robbery between the weddings of my two children.

The death of a child is not on par with any of those events and it is absurd to even think it is.

According to Silverman and Rubin[33], from the 1980s to the present, evidence has changed the way we think about bereavement and mourning. The time frame in which bereavement is an active factor in people's lives has changed from days and weeks to months and years.

---

[33] https://onlinelibrary.wiley.com/doi/10.1002/9781118625392.wb ecp239

Attitudes have changed. No longer are the bereaved advised to 'let go', 'get on with things'. We don't recover, we don't get over it. We become different. While the death is an event, grief is not. Grief is a process.

I am a walking wounded just like you are, yet I am stronger now. No personal quality is more central to mourning the death of your child than courage.

BUT MY HEART IS TOO FULL OF PAIN

Of course, your heart is too full of pain. Yet your heart has the wonderful ability to grow.

For those of us who gave birth to more than one child – remember how you made room in your heart for each additional child.

Remember when each grandchild was born? Your heart swelled yet again.

There will always be a place in your heart for your beloved child. The memories of your loved one will always be there. In due time, painful reminiscing of your beloved child will give ways to pleasant memories.

GO EASY ON YOURSELF

Grief is a whole life process. There will be days when you feel you do not want to survive. The pain is unbearable, and you want nothing more than to be reunited with your child. This is a normal reaction. One day in the future you will feel that life is worth living again. For now, think of how important you are to your partner, your remaining children, your own parents and your friends.

Each one of us has an individual style of coping with painful experiences. Some of the ways to help you manage your feelings of grief are to talk with family and friends, seek counselling, exercise, eat healthily, seek spiritual support, take time to relax, listen to music or join a support group. The most important things to do are to allow yourself to feel grief and to be patient with yourself

FACTORS AFFECTING COPING

There are many factors that will affect your coping ability. These include your own personality and health, your coping ability in general, your upbringing, your support system and whatever else is currently happening in your life, together with family and friends.

What was your relationship with your child? Were they living at home, or independently – nearby, or overseas? Was the death sudden, violent, or after a prolonged, incurable illness?

Are there other children in the home? Older or younger? Are there aged grandparents struggling to deal with this death while they feel it should have been them, whose days are numbered?

Other factors include what else you have experienced in your life, your daily and past struggles and any previous experience you had with death or other hardships.

Your financial circumstances may also affect your coping ability. Can you stay at home and slowly try to learn to adapt to the loss – or do you have to race back to work?

Some people find comfort through their faith in G-d. Some people, like myself, find it useful to believe in G-d because it provides me with the opportunity to blame someone for allowing Danny to get sick in the first place.

My parents and parents-in-law had all died before Danny was diagnosed, so I was experienced with death. However, it shook me to my core when Danny was diagnosed with his fatal cancer three days after my mother's funeral.

My upbringing was such that after the death of a parent, among other restrictions I should not listen to music for one year. As I am not a great fan of music, this was hardly a sacrifice. However, I desperately needed this distraction to take my mind off the possibility, indeed the probability, of Danny's premature death.

Your level of spirituality and belief in the after-life will also play a part in your coping ability. For me, death is no longer a fear. Several years ago I had my own episode with cancer and was not scared at all by the possibility of death. How can I be scared of a place where my child is residing?

I do feel sorry for a bereaved mother I know who does not believe in the hereafter. For her, life after death is – splat! Over. Finished. I think that is so sad, not feeling that there would be any connection with her beloved son.

Watching friends, once playmates of your child, growing up, going through all of life's celebrations with their own children, may be hard.

Life as we knew it has changed. We must build a wall to protect our fragile state of mind and strengthen us, so we can carry on with the rituals of daily life.

What are the rules? There are no rules, no such thing as 'grief etiquette', no expectations, no right or wrong ways.

Your relationship with your beloved child

It does not matter what age your child was at death – you will still miss that child all your life.

Thank G-d I never had a miscarriage or a stillborn child. I think to have all your dreams shattered at the height of joy and anticipation of a new life would be devastating. Currently in Australia there is a support group for Jewish couples called Tefilat-Chana providing support for infertility, pregnancy loss and reproductive health issues.[34]

For the first couple of years we take our new infant with us wherever we go. They are a part of our life twenty-four hours a day, when we go shopping, visit friends or chauffeur our other children here and there. We get alarmed if we hear them in the night and are attentive to every cough and sniffle. Now suddenly, that link is gone. We spent six months, one year or two, listening to every sound that came from this child, watching every action and suddenly, it is all over. Our role has been eradicated.

A slightly older child is a vital part of your daily routine. They have their own place in the family, their own personality such as the quiet one, the studious one, the one who loses things, never does homework, hates vegetables, excels in sport. You are in charge of their food, clothes, homework, sporting activities and rosters.

As they develop into teenagers, they try to assert their independence. They have their own friends and interests, but you are still a major force in their lives and involved in most aspects of their daily routines.

Once your child reaches adulthood and leaves home, there is a different scenario. You speak to them regularly.

---

[34] www.tefilatchana.org.

They may live nearby, or in another country and you are no longer responsible for their daily needs. Their death may be leaving behind a grieving widow and fatherless children.

ACCEPTING WORDS OF SYMPATHY

We have all had well-meaning friends make unsuitable, hurtful comments.

I have heard some of the most bizarre:

'At least the younger son does not have to compete with his big brother now'
'Well, you won't have the expense of a wedding now'
'He died doing what he loved'
'He would not want you to cry'
'At least you have other children'
'You are young – you can have more children'

Seemingly innocent remarks comparing the death of your child to someone's father, uncle, wife or beloved pet come across as absurd and rather insulting.

I can say 'At least he is not in pain any more' about my beloved child. I knew his pain. With every breath in my body I felt his suffering. But it is not up to anyone else to make that comment.

However, a part of growing and accepting the death of our child is to accept such comments, acknowledging that it is the thought that counts not necessarily the words.

These people are not going out of their way to hurt us. They are trying their best to offer some consolation. They simply do not understand the unfathomable depth of our loss and how it will affect us for the rest of our life.

ADVICE TO FRIENDS

My daughter, Renée, received the following passage from a friend after Danny died. My husband found it useful to give to friends when he could not sufficiently express himself.

What Grieving people REALLY want you to understand

"I'm just numb and I will not recover from my loss. This is not a cold or the flu. I'm not sick. I'm grieving and that's different. I will not always be grieving as intensely, but I will never forget my loved one and rather than recover, I want to incorporate his life and love into the rest of my life. That person is part of me and always will be, and sometimes I will remember him with joy and other times with a tear. Both are normal.

I must accept the death. Yes, I have to understand that it has happened and it is real, but there are just some things in life that are not fair.

Please don't avoid me. You can't catch my grief. My world is painful, and when you are too afraid to call me or visit or say anything, you isolate me at a time when I most need to be thought about.

Please don't say, 'Call me if you need anything.' I'll never call you because I have no idea what I need.

When you tell me what I should be doing I feel even more lost and alone. I feel bad enough that my loved one is dead, so please don't make it worse by telling me I'm not doing this right.

I don't even understand what you mean when you say, 'You've got to get on with your life.' My life is going on, but it may not look the way you think it should. This will take time and I never will be my old self again. So please, just accept me as I am, and I hope with your support some normality will slowly return to my life. But I will never forget and there will always be times that I cry.

Remember you're on the outside looking in. To assume that I've moved on and am back to 'normal' is absolutely wrong. I'm living."

GUIDEPOSTS[35]

Each day will have its challenges, but as you look at the awesome task ahead – how to negotiate the pitfalls and anticipate some of the hazards in the valley of the shadow of death – these are some of the things you might try to learn:

1. Do those things that give you peace of mind; not necessarily what others suggest or pressure you to do.

2. Surround yourself with people who understand and make you feel comfortable, who know they cannot fix things, who are compassionate and who do not try to take your grief away from you.

3. Tell those who care about you what you need to survive (they do not automatically know) and accept the fact that not all relatives and old friends will be able to provide what you need at this time. You may have to give some of them up.

4. Give yourself permission to do what you feel like doing, as long as you harm no one: cry alone, pray, scream, cry

---

[35] Reproduced from www.shiva.com. Permission to use was obtained.

with others, withdraw, express anger, meditate, cry some more.

5. Grieve when and how you want to, rather than on someone else's timetable.

6. Do things at your own pace, in accordance with your own feelings and accept the idea that you may not be able to accomplish everything you used to – at least for now, though perhaps long-term as well.

7. Maintain open communication with your spouse and children, recognizing that we each grieve differently.

8. Do not ignore your own needs. This is one time of life when it is okay to be selfish sometimes.

9. Try hard to believe that life really is worth living, whether your rationale be to perpetuate your child's memory, or to resume accomplishing the goals you previously had set for yourself, or to strive toward entirely new goals, or to try to find the answers to the age-old question of 'Why?' Or for any other reason that has meaning to you.

10. Have faith, even on the darkest days, that there will indeed be light at the end of the tunnel, that life may again have meaning as you begin to emerge from the valley of the shadow.

RELATIONSHIPS

We bereaved are not alone. We belong to the largest company in all the world – the company of those who have known suffering.　***Helen Keller***

DO RELATIONSHIPS CHANGE?

You bet they do! Firstly, for those widowed or divorced, with no other half to turn to – I know it is hard, but don't assume it is all that easy for a couple either.

Grief is a very personal journey. It may be hard for husband and wife, both suffering, to give support to each other. Men and women grieve differently, every individual grieves differently, but it is important to support each other, accept differences and respect each other's feelings.

The main advice is to try to help each other and keep the family united.

In our case, sadly I knew the facts. I knew the inevitable while my husband was adamant that 'while there is life, there is hope!' When Danny died my husband pretty much went into shock, whereas I had begun mourning when the cancer was diagnosed.

Maybe your child was married and he or she has left behind a young widow or widower, and your grandchildren. Falling in love, getting married and having a family was the trifecta Danny never thought he would win, but he did. He was immensely proud of his family. Three years later, my daughter-in-law was a young widow, sole breadwinner, sole parent. And the primary link I had with her – my son – was now gone.

How does one feel and cope when the daughter-in-law remarries and moves interstate, as happened to me? And your grandchild is now living 3,500 kilometres away and may now be calling another man 'Daddy'. I am grateful that I have a happy relationship with my daughter-in-law and am in constant touch with my granddaughter.

It is so very hard to navigate through these challenges in this new life of yours. At least in our support group we have others who have gone through all these experiences, and more. We can share our knowledge and journeys, our mistakes and our successes.

WHAT ABOUT FRIENDSHIPS?

At a time when you are the most vulnerable you have ever been, you may find that you have the task of educating others. This may seem highly unfair and often overwhelming, but the reality is that some people have limited experience with death and little understanding of the grieving process you are going through.

Some friends will go out of their way – some to help, some to avoid you! But try not to be bitter. Do not harbour resentment. You have enough to deal with.

I am happy with friends I can talk to about Danny, although I know some feel uncomfortable about it at times. But often I press on regardless and find that they overcome their discomfort.

FAMILY DYNAMICS

Your family will never be the same unit of individuals again and each member is affected differently. It may be hard for husband and wife to give support to each other, likewise for a grieving parent to help the other children. But you must do whatever you can to avoid deterioration of your fractured family, while still taking care of yourself.

I feel deeply for those who had only one child or those who lost all their children and who question if they are still a parent. Of course you are. Once you have become a parent you are always one, even though there may no longer be a child to love and nurture. It is important that you reach out to other family members, make new friends and immortalise your child/ren the best way you can. There is an international support group set up in America called Alive Alone[36]. They have some very good articles for parents dealing with the death of an only child or all their children.

SPOUSE

As I have pointed out many times, grief is a personal journey and individuals react in different ways. One may need to talk while the other opts to grieve in silence; one withdraws from the world, the other works long hours. One partner can bring the other one down. One's better day can coincide with the other's bad day. But try to support each other, accept differences and honour each other's feelings. And talk! It is possible to learn new

---

[36] www.alivealone.org

things about each other, help with weaknesses and benefit from strengths.

The indescribable pain and pressure you feel in the wake of your child's death is shared by your spouse. When you express your despair by lashing out at the world, the nearest and easiest target is your mate. Anger or blame directed at your spouse can endanger the strongest of marriages. In the face of overwhelming grief, it is vital that a couple give each other space when needed. A couple must consciously resolve to be honest with each other about how they feel, but also protect each other and be sensitive to the spouse's needs.

Tolerance, affection, honesty, patience and good communication are vital to maintaining a good relationship.

THE SINGLE PARENT

While it may be hard seeing your partner suffering as much as you are, it may be even harder when there is no one to whom you can turn. I refer here to widows/widowers, divorced and single parents.

There may be no one with whom to share the worst hours of the day and night. These are times when you really need to find comfort, be it a friend, a professional or a support group. You need not grieve alone. If you always hide away, you deprive yourself of the opportunity to be comforted.

A word of caution: if you have other children, try not to lean on them too much. Some may be very supporting and accommodating, but others may find it overpowering – they have lost a sibling and they have their own life to live. A child, now the only one, may feel an extra burden of responsibility for his bereaved parent, as if he must draw from a limitless supply of strength.

DAUGHTER-IN-LAW/SON-IN-LAW

Regardless of what happens further down the track, at this moment your married child's widow/widower is next of kin to the deceased, the one with forms to fill in and people to notify. Your daughter-in-law or son-in-law now must perform whatever household and administrative tasks their partner did, while looking after their children, largely on their own. Also, their social structure has changed – they are now the odd one out.

Apart from the grief they are enduring, the spontaneity of their life has gone and their income has been affected. They may feel alone and frightened as full responsibility for any children falls on their shoulders alone.

Be compassionate. Go easy on each other. Your daughter or son-in-law is suffering too.

SURVIVING CHILD/REN

A parent is often so consumed by grief that he loses sight of the needs of surviving siblings. A youngster may feel that he must wade through a morass of unresolved feelings without parental support. In losing a brother or sister, their playmate, children may also, in a sense, lose their parents. As overwhelmed as you are in your own grief, surviving children must become the upper-most concern, almost beyond your own grief. It is vital not to allow a grieving child to feel alone.

Do not hide your own grief and encourage them to express their sorrow. Let them know that although it is not the same, you both share the grief.

The siblings also may not realise their own importance and need to be reassured that their parents' grief would be just as intense if they were the one who had died.

Ensure the children do not harbour any feelings of guilt, like having been mean or fighting with their sibling. Try to explain as naturally as possible that there is a lot we do not understand about death, and repeatedly emphasise that death is beyond anyone's control. Do not avoid talking about your deceased child with his or her siblings. Your child existed and his or her siblings need to feel free to express their feelings and questions too, without fear of upsetting you.

Having had the first-hand experience of their sibling's death, their easy sense of innocence – their belief that they are safe and will always be taken care of – has been shattered. They have become aware that their parents cannot always protect them. They may also fear dying like their brother or sister did, so they need facts – within their ability to understand – so their fear does not grow out of proportion. Assure them it is not contagious.

Sibling status

I have mentioned it before. Try not to lean too heavily on your remaining children, especially if there is just the one.

This child may have now attained the role of being the only child and all the responsibilities this entails, feeling an obligation to lighten the burden of their grieving bereaved parents, whist grieving themselves.

The opposite scenario is also true. Be aware of the extreme of wrapping remaining children in cotton-wool, being over protective of them.

Each child now has a different place in the family circle. The sibling they looked up to, or the younger one they helped to look after, is no longer there. Family routines, responsibilities and chores may change. Be very aware of the effect this has on each surviving child.

Young children

What to tell younger children depends on the age of child, circumstances of death, and the individual child. I have read that children aged five can understand that death is final but may still question if the deceased can eat or move, while a seven-year-old, in our TV and internet society, understands it better. Of course, this depends on the child.

It is important to know just what level of understanding your youngsters have. I read about a little boy who was told his brother is now an angel, so the sibling began to misbehave as he did not want G-d to take him also.

Teenagers

This is a time when their lives are filled with stress and confusion, their bodies are changing, their awareness of the world is changing, their views, their sense of responsibility – and now this!

At a time of their lives when they should be growing in self confidence, they lose their sense of invincibility instead. While they didn't think themselves immortal – they were certain of some permanents in their life. And now that has been trampled!

If it is hard for us as adults to understand, how much more so for a teenager. Suddenly they are a part of changed family dynamics. Maybe they are feeling ignored, having lost their own sibling, their best friend, their confidante. Who can they turn to? Surely none of their friends will understand their grief.

Sometimes adding to this grief may be the cruelty of peers (intentional or unintentional). Your teenage children may feel they have to be strong. They do not want to add to your distress. It is important that they know they can discuss their feelings with you, and you can offer support to each other.

Adult children

Our adult children have their own lives to live. They have, in most cases, established themselves in a relationship, a career and a certain lifestyle. They grieve the death of their sibling, but they must also care for their partner and their own children.

My daughter Renée was seven months' pregnant with her second child when Danny died. Two months later she was encumbered in the usual chaos of sleepless nights and a crying baby, together with a toddler. I still wonder if she had a chance to fully mourn for her brother.

Again, I stress it is important that we do not lean too much on our remaining children, that we let them live their lives. They will never forget their sibling. The grief will be with them all their life, just as it is with you.

Avoid the pedestal

Try not to compare the child who survives with the one who died. Surviving children often feel they cannot live up to the parents' ideal of the dead child and may start to resent him, then rebel, feeling inadequate.

Sometimes too, surviving children feel they must be 'both children' for you. Be careful that this does not occur.

YOUR PARENTS

If your parents are alive then spare a thought for them too. These grandparents have lost a grandchild and are also seeing their own child suffering. They are experiencing a double loss and are struggling too.

Also, just as we might think, 'Why my child, it should have been me?' some grandparents wonder why they are still alive while their young grandchild was taken so early.

Just as you want to make things better for your remaining children, so too does a grandparent ache for your loss. Their often profound grief is underestimated, and they are generally given little attention.

One grandmother approached me because she was concerned about her daughter's prolonged mourning for her young child. This grandmother not only lost a grandchild but was watching her daughter struggling and the effect it was having on the rest of the family. Another grandmother is distraught over the effect the death of her grandchild is having on her son. Unfortunately, her husband prefers not to talk about it.

GRANDCHILD/REN

Your grandchild has lost a parent. The other parent is in constant tears and although you help as much as you can, they are suddenly living the life of a sole parent. They are grieving, probably tired and short-tempered.

Although you too are suffering, try to lend a hand to help and stay actively involved with your grandchildren. They have lost a parent and there are so many stories that only you can tell them about their beloved parent, to keep the memory alive for you and them. You will find that you and your grandchild/ren can laugh together over some of the stories you recall about things your child got up to when he or she was young. This also allows your grandchildren the freedom to ask questions and talk about their mother or father, rather than being afraid to mention him or her for fear of hurting you, or their surviving parent.

I have completed a 'Family Roots' project for my granddaughter with as much information as I can about Danny and his ancestors.

There are some issues that may arise regarding grandchildren. It helps to be able to talk with other parents who have dealt with these and other matters unique to our circumstances.

OTHER FAMILY MEMBERS

Aunts and uncles, nieces and nephews, your siblings and cousins – many will go on with their lives without any change.

Some may offer unwavering support but let you down while others will genuinely be there for you.

You will learn who is there for you, who cares for you long after the official period of mourning has passed, but they may not always know how to help you. Tell them. Stay in touch with them. Be a part of each other's lives.

FRIENDS AND COLLEAGUES

At a time when you are the most vulnerable, you may find that you have the task of educating others. This may seem highly unfair, often overwhelming, but the reality is that some people have limited experience with death and have little understanding of the grieving process that you are going through.

FRIENDS – OLD AND NEW

Some friends will stay away, some will offend. Some will ask if you are getting on with your life and if you have found closure. There is no such thing following the death of your child.

People can say stupid things – even your best friends and family members. They can also be unpredictable. Some will surprise you by the extent of their thoughtfulness while others will astound you by their total lack of consideration.

It may be hard accepting words of sympathy – but remember it's the thought that counts, not necessarily the words.

I have an old friend. Our children grew up together. She is not religious but is a traditional Jew in a very broad sense of the word. She drove thirty kilometres most days during the *shiva* period and sat at the back of the room, hardly saying a word. Later, she told me she was speechless. She knew there was nothing she could say to lessen my pain but wanted me to know she was there for me.

Sometimes your friends want to help but do not know how. Ask them, call them, talk to them. Let them know. Sometimes even your closest friends are afraid to do or say the wrong thing. They certainly do not mean it. They are trying to offer words of comfort. It is hard and you are at your most fragile – but try not to take offence if they say the wrong thing.

Do not feel uncomfortable about your heightened dependence on friends right now. Take comfort in the knowledge that they care about you.

Some friends have a way with words that may upset you. Politely explain if they do so.

I have another old friend with whom we often holidayed with our families. She found Danny's death 'too hard to deal with' and we lost contact. When we passed in the street there was a polite smile of recognition. I have stopped smiling back. Interestingly she is also friends with two other families who have since suffered a similar loss. I wonder if my friend is coping better now.

There are newly bereaved mothers who, in the early days go out of the area to do the shopping to avoid being seen or to prevent others from changing direction when seeing you and not knowing what to say.

Sometimes people find that former friends and acquaintances do not invite them over any more or seem to avoid speaking to them. But many also discover warmth and kindness in the most unexpected places and from people they may not even know very well.

Realise that your friends' lives are going on as usual. Friends may have issues they don't like to bother you with because they realise their catastrophe is insignificant in comparison to yours. It may well be insignificant compared to what has happened in your life, but try to remember that for your friend, finding a silver pair of shoes that fit, or where to get the best hair treatment is important to her at this time. It is not easy at first, but after a while, try to re-enter your friend's life. Some people are special and you do not want to lose their friendship.

NEW FRIENDSHIPS

After the death of a child, it is important that we do not isolate ourselves and lose touch with society. It may help to develop new interests and meet new friends. I surprised myself by not only attending a U3A course on my own, but also by corralling a small group of my new-found friends to meet for the occasional lunch date. I used to be the most shy and insecure kid on the block!

New friends are indeed like a breath of fresh air. It is a new beginning. Of course, you have not left behind the reminiscences of your child – it is therapeutic to tell a new listener about your child as you relive those precious memories.

You may be surprised to hear that your friend also has a sad story to share and you venture into your new relationship as kindred spirits.

COLLEAGUES

If you are in the workforce your relationship with your colleagues is important. The first weeks back at your old job may be uncomfortable. Workmates may be wary for fear of saying the wrong thing and it may be up to you to make them feel comfortable to talk to you.

After a few weeks pass, your loss becomes history for them and you may be greeted with the generic 'How're you going, mate?' or 'Did you have a good weekend?'

Note also that your colleagues are generally not part of your social circle. They might not know you personally and vice-versa. With the multi-cultural society we have now, they may have experienced many personal losses of which you are not aware. They may have escaped genocide in their former country or other forms of persecution.

Try to be open-minded. Accept their condolences with the spirit in which they are given, and do not be offended if they say something that upsets you.

<u>SEEKING HELP</u>

Your grief is your own. But you need not grieve alone.

Most of us will rejoin society over time. It does take time, and everyone has to find their own path. Go easy on yourself – the most important thing is that you give yourself time to grieve. There is no such thing as grief etiquette, there are no rules, no expectations and no right or wrong ways to grieve.

ACCEPTING HELP FROM OTHERS

Some people may offer you support. Other bereaved parents may offer support. Take it. Do not be afraid to reach out and ask people for help. At times I have offered support to newly bereaved parents who say they don't want to burden me further. Truly – I would not offer to help unless I wanted to. But I and others like me do not want to become a nuisance and keep offering – so please, if you want help and it has been offered, then accept it.

It is said that the single most important factor in healing from loss is having the support of other people. Even if you are not comfortable talking about your feelings under normal circumstances, some people, (mainly intuitive grievers[37]) may feel the need to express them when you are grieving, although others (instrumental

---

[37] Refer to section Intuitive and instrumental grievers , page 32

grievers) may benefit from doing something with their support network and not actively share their grief.

I know it may sound odd, impossible or somehow illogical – as if discussing the death of your beloved child with someone will make you hurt less. You may even feel that you are betraying your child by hoping that telling your story will dissipate your grief a little. But be assured – it is definitely not like that. Sharing your loss just makes the burden of grief easier to carry. Wherever the support comes from, accept it and do not grieve alone. Connecting to others will help you heal.

Turn to friends and family members. Now is the time to lean on the people who care about you, even if you usually take pride in being strong and self-sufficient. Make an effort to draw loved ones closer rather than avoiding them and accept the assistance that is offered. Often people want to help but do not know how, so tell them what you need – whatever it is.

Intuitive grievers, who grieve from the heart, may benefit from a support group. Grief can feel very lonely, even when you have loved ones around. Sharing your sorrow with others who have experienced similar losses can help. Strangely enough, you may even find you are able to share laughter with these parents who know what you are feeling. That laughter does not mean that you do not feel grief. There is no judgement in a support group.

Instrumental grievers won't want to sit around and share their stories. From my husband's own experience with the JBP support group, several attempts at breakfast meetings or supper nights were unsuccessful. But when the opportunity arose for the men to attend a private *shiur* (learning session) over ten men attended, so those in mourning still were able to say *Kaddish*, supported by a room full of other bereaved fathers.

Some people feel the need to be more in touch with G-d at this time, while others feel rejected. You may find a great support to draw comfort from your Judaism, or the simple concept of a 'higher being' if you can, regardless of your level of commitment. Having said that, and after many years of reflection, I have mixed feelings towards G-d. Having prayed fervently for Danny's survival for ten years I feel that G-d did not listen to me. Some may say He prolonged Danny's life for ten years. Whatever the reason, I acknowledge that I do believe in G-d, but I am not happy with him!

Some people may find comfort in music, mediation, art or exercise. Seek out whatever works best for you.

COUNSELLING

I know many people see a counsellor and it helps them. Personally, I saw various counsellors throughout Danny's illness and none of them helped, so this does not strike a positive chord with me, though others have benefitted from it immensely.

Many will disagree, but I find it hard to imagine that someone who has not personally experienced the death of a child can really understand the depth of despair a bereaved parent endures.

But, it is imperative to have someone to talk to – if you can find the right person. Ask around, shop around and find someone you can relate to and with whom you feel comfortable and confident.

I must point out that my situation, how I felt and reacted and continue to react, having had a child with a terminal illness for ten years, is vastly different from those whose child died suddenly, unexpectedly.

Through the registry which I created for people with Danny's rare cancer, I came across numerous people whose condition was precarious. Over those ten years quite a few members died. I remember a girl, Danny's age, asking me if I wanted her mum to let me know when she died. I spoke to many such parents and spouses over those years. Somehow when Danny died, I felt I did not need someone who had not gone through what I had to tell me how to deal with Danny's death.

But having said that, I do have a wonderful GP who might not be able to comfort me over my loss but has become a valued confidante. I always benefit from chatting with her.

Also, I now know of several very good professionals in Melbourne and Sydney who specialise in grief support.

There are a few other forms of counselling you can pursue. The Australian Centre for Grief and Bereavement[38] can put you in touch with a qualified grief counsellor to see either at their premises (at a reduced rate) or others in private practice.

The Compassionate Friends of Victoria[39] have a variety of support groups as well as regular workshops. They also have twenty-four-hour telephone support, manned by volunteers who are all bereaved parents.

There are other organisations that offer support, but I have no experience with them. These include Beyond

---

[38] Situated in Mulgrave, Melbourne, Phone 03 92652100, website www.grief.org.au

[39] Situated in Canterbury, Melbourne, Phone 03 9888 4944, www.compassionatefriendsvictoria.org.au

Blue, Lifeline, Anglicare, Sids & Kids. I have also been informed that Jesuit Social Services run an excellent program for those grieving the death of a child from suicide.

One size does not fit all

The knowledge of a counsellor comes from studying, listening and observing, while that from a fellow bereaved parent comes from their suffering. It does help to talk to somebody – if you can find the right person.

Personally, I did not have much luck with professionals while Danny was sick – the only one who was great was a palliative care oncologist at Peter MacCallum Cancer Hospital, with whom both Danny and I had a relationship – and he made *Aliyah*!

Medical experts tell us that grief is a natural part of the healing process after a significant loss, such as loss of a loved one, the loss of health, or letting go of a long-held dream. They even include other factors such as leaving home, death of a pet, change of job, loss of physical ability or loss of financial security. No way! Anyone who has suffered the death of a child will emphatically inform the 'experts' that they would happily swap their loss of a job, or a limb, or all their money – to have their child back in their lives.

Some 'experts' who enter the grief profession may do so because they have endured a life-changing loss and feel that they can be empathetic. Yet, I remember when Danny was ill, seeing a grief counsellor at a well-known hospital who was helping parents deal with the issues of seriously ill kids. I spent three sessions with this professional while she walked up and down the room 'trying to empathise with what it would be like having a child riddled with cancer'. For goodness sake! Isn't that why I was referred to her!

Based on my own experiences I have been quite critical of counsellors but in the process of researching this book, I have come across some professionals I highly recommend, and who have opened my eyes to the value of trained professionals.

For many years I suffered from debilitating panic attacks. It was only after my mother, and then Danny, got cancer and I had to sit through very traumatic consultations, that I was able to put those fears aside (and replace them with anxiety about my mum's health, and then Danny's). The professional I consulted had trained to deal with people suffering from panic attacks by inventing an exercise where the patient felt like everyone was looking at him, making him feel horribly self-conscious. He went to the movies, sat in one of the front rows and just before the movie was about to start he stood up, turned to face the rest of the audience, told them the ending of the movie then sat down! To make things worse, as they were leaving his wife had to go to the bathroom while he waited outside – the movie goers walking past giving him nasty glares!

So, yes, I believe he did understand a bit about my panic attacks.

SHULE

Embrace the comfort of the mourning rituals that your *shule* can provide. Spiritual activities that are meaningful to you may help. If you are questioning religion, try talking to your rabbi or someone who can help you reconnect. Belonging to a *shule* and being part of that community may provide much needed spiritual support.

A highly-qualified and well-respected grief counsellor held some workshops in Melbourne with a group of rabbis, advising them on how to deal with bereaved families. Ask your rabbi about this or contact me for more information.

I must admit that I do not get comfort from going to *shule*, in fact, quite the opposite. I know Danny is in a better place. I know there is some part of him that exists, presumably in heaven. I suppose there must be someone in charge and I guess that would be G-d. Yes, I do believe that G-d exists, but I find it very painful to go to *shule* because I feel like my attendance shows G-d that I am okay with His decision to allow Danny to have got cancer and subsequently die.

SUPPORT GROUPS

A support group affirms that your experiences and feelings are normal. To suddenly discover that others have the same reactions to certain things can be liberating. Role models can be important too. Seeing others like you who can get on with things, such as helping others, gives hope and encouragement.

Secondly, grievers tend to feel isolated and alone in their grief. To look into tearful eyes across a table and hear someone say, 'I understand', and know they really do, lessens the loneliness. Being in a support group may help you to accept and work through your grief.

Many bereaved parents emphasise the importance of connecting with other people who share their pain. The things these people can offer – their willingness to listen to you, their respect and total understanding of your pain, their faith in your ability to heal and move forward – these provide a foundation upon which you can begin the long and difficult process of rebuilding your life without your child.

In an article *Bereavement/Grief Interventions*[40] P R Silverman states that whether in professionally led groups or in groups formed by the bereaved themselves, the bereaved learn from and support each other to cope with their loss, building on experiential knowledge. The strengths and experiences of shared experiences are fully recognised.

After the initial early response to grief and offers to help, relatives and friends usually begin to pick up their own lives. Parents are left to deal with their grief alone. But those who have compassion, those who have been hurt by similar pain, seek to accompany those newly bereaved offering a presence of understanding. You feel so alone when your child has died, so singled out by adverse fate, so bereft in a world of happy, intact families. Then you join a support group and realise how many other people like you there are out there. Being in a group helps newly bereaved parents by being with others who understand, seeing how others have coped and created a changed life.

I have met quite a few bereaved people who at the mention of a support group, or even the fact that they might be interested – totally clammed up. Sadly, they have buried their memories of their loved one together with the child himself, for fear of enduring painful

---

[40] Phyllis R Silverman is a researcher teacher and author whose main interest is bereavement and how death is dealt with in our society. This article was published online in *The Encyclopedia of Clinical Psychology*, 2015

thoughts. I feel so sorry that they cannot reflect on the joy that their child brought into their lives.

I am not pushing, promoting or in any way trying to advance Jewish Bereaved Parents support group. But if you are in Melbourne, please think about contacting us. Contrary to regular bereavement support groups, we encourage our members to develop other interests. We provide exercise classes, outings, a Scrabble group, craft activities, lunches, a book club and more. After many of these activities we sit back and chat, and then introduce whatever issues are concerning us about our loss and ongoing issues. These are generally women-only functions. The men have their own meetings.

I am continually struck by the power of the bond between bereaved parents. Strangers become friends and confidantes in a very short time. No matter our circumstances, who we are or how different we are, there is no greater bond than the connection between parents who understand the agony of enduring the death of a child. It's a pain we suffer for a lifetime. Unfortunately, only those who have walked the path of child-loss understand the depth and breadth of both the pain and the love we carry.

REBUILDING YOUR LIFE

"The reality is that we don't forget, move on, and have closure, but rather we honour, we remember, and incorporate our deceased children and siblings into our lives in a new way. In fact, keeping memories of your loved one alive in your mind and heart is an important part of your healing journey." **– Harriet Schiff, author of *The Bereaved Parent***

Bitter or better – we can choose to wallow in the pain of our loss and indeed for the first year, two years, three, four or five years, this may be all we can do.

But there should come a time when we can turn from mourning to other tasks, to thinking of others, to reaching out to the sick, the elderly, the vulnerable, to helping newly bereaved parents – and as we do this we realise we are doing it in honour of our beloved child. He or she is the impetus for our reaching out to help others. And we smile. And we can be proud of ourselves. And proud of our sons and daughters because it is through our love for them that we are reaching out, it is in their name.

Our children are now our teachers. I ask myself, 'What would Danny want me to do?' He is my guiding light, my connection to G-d. He is my conscience.

THE FIRST YEAR

The death of your child has affected you deeply and spiritually. What you once thought provided meaning and purpose to your life may now leave you feeling empty. You are faced with the daunting task of redefining for yourself the values and convictions that will help you to move forward without the physical presence of your child. For many of you, your belief in G-d will sustain you as you grapple with the very mystery of life – that part of it we cannot understand but somehow struggle courageously to accept.

Your overall lifestyle may change also, depending on the age of your beloved child when they died.

There is no moving on – there is only moving forward. From the time death touches our lives we move forward; we are given no other choice than to move forward. However, we never get to a place where the words 'move on' resonate. These words, 'move on', have a negative connotation to the grieving. They suggest a closure that is non-existent and a fictitious door we pass through.

For those of us living in the Jewish ghetto, be it Caulfield or wherever, there is an issue of everybody knowing everybody. I remember one of my first outings many months after Danny died, sitting in Glick's cafe and someone walked in and acknowledged me. I said to my friend, also a bereaved mother, 'Do I know him?' She replied, 'Maybe not, but he probably knows about Danny's death and that you are his mother.'

'HOW ARE YOU?' GRR!!

I used to get extremely upset when people asked me this, but I acknowledge it really is just a universal greeting, like when a shop assistant asks the same question.

Recently a fellow bereaved mum told me she was upset that, while attending a gathering an old acquaintance approached her and complimented her on her outfit. I asked her would she have preferred if her acquaintance asked, 'How are you?' Her friend was trying to be thoughtful by approaching her. She could have said nothing or avoided her completely.

Sometimes it is hard to know what you want from others!

ONE DAY AT A TIME

When Danny was diagnosed with his fatal cancer, I was told I was mourning prematurely and advised I should take things 'one day at a time'.

I printed out this mantra and stuck it wherever I could. And yes, it did help, momentarily, to calm me down.

You have suffered an enormous blow. You may feel that you will never recover. Your journey of grief will be a lifelong process, but you will move forward gradually.

Be patient – take things one day at a time.

NO MAJOR DECISIONS AT THIS TIME

Grief can cloud your thought processes and if you make abrupt decisions you may regret them later. Many experts suggest waiting for at least six months to a year before moving, changing jobs, clearing out keepsakes and making other momentous decisions, allowing you to experience all the seasons of your emotions.

One of the many challenging aspects of grieving the death of a child who was living at home, is the possessions they leave behind. What do you keep? What do you throw away? When?

Some people choose to leave their child's room untouched, some people just keep a few keepsakes and other reminders. Beware! Once discarded, these irreplaceable mementos can never be replaced.

Danny was married and living in his own home when he died. I believe my daughter-in-law made a wise decision several months after Danny died, when there was an appeal for clothing for people who lost their homes and all their possessions in the Lake Mountain bushfires. This provided her with an opportunity to 'let go' of a lot of Danny's clothing.

THE JEWISH FESTIVALS AND *SIMCHAS*

Danny died on 6 September 2008, a week before *Rosh Hashanah*. For the previous ten years I prayed in *shule*, 'On *Rosh Hashanah* it will be inscribed, and on *Yom Kippur* it will be sealed: How many shall pass on and how many shall be born; who will live and who will die; who will die at his predestined time and who before his time.'

I know the explanation to this is not as simple as it appears. There is a detailed explanation in the collection of inspirational writings at the end of this book. Nonetheless, for a mother praying for a sick son, year in and year out, and then for him to die – makes me feel that my prayers were unanswered.

From the end of July each year, I dread turning over the pages of the calendar. I don't even need to look. Everyone starts the countdown, 'It's *Yomtov* in only six weeks', 'It's *Yomtov* in four weeks', 'Where are you going for *Yomtov*?'. Enough already! I don't want to hear about it. And suddenly, it is getting closer. 'It's *Yomtov* in just two weeks'. And I know that it's *Yahrzeit* for Danny in just a few days' time. I turn over the pages of the calendar and see the dreaded date in print, 22 *Elul*. And the panic sets in.

The *Yomtovim* are always so hard and can't always be avoided. I know our *seders* will never be the same. It used to be a mini-celebration, with the extended family, including my nephews, Danny's cousins – the ones he fought with to see who could sing the loudest, or finish *Eichad Mi Yodeah* the quickest. I am delighted that these young men are now successful, proud family men, but it hurts!

This year I cried over the beautiful silver *seder* plate, now in our possession, that Danny received as a wedding present, together with a cherished bookmark he made in Prep, the *matzah* cover in Grade 1 and the *afikomen* bag in Grade 2.

Actually, I was a wreck! I contacted some of my dear friends from the support group – one whose son didn't reach adulthood, one who doesn't get to have any contact with her grandchildren, one whose grandchild sits with the new step-parent at *Bubba's seder* table.

I remembered two other friends whose children died during the week of *Pesach*.

I try to be strong, go back to my normal thinking, happy we had Danny in our lives for twenty-nine years – but at times like these it is so hard to stop the tears from falling.

For many years I felt like I was being hit with a sledge hammer every time someone wished me 'good Yomtov'. It seemed unavoidable and aggravated me wherever I turned – in shops, on Facebook, in emails and texts. After a while I realised I had to start acknowledging these sentiments and wish the same to others, but I admit in the earlier days that I did it without sincerity.

And still I have friends, no matter how well they seem to know me, who cannot understand how hard it is for me to 'celebrate' *Yomtov*! There is no joy in it for me, none whatsoever!

Last year we invited my niece and her family to join us. My niece was orphaned when she was nineteen, some twenty-odd years ago. My daughter brought several bottles of an Israeli-make of strawberry and banana juice. This was Danny's favourite and we had not indulged in years. Yuk! It was so sweet. But we all persevered and drank a glass in memory of Danny at the *seder*. We also laughed at the fact that we bought it locally whereas fifteen and twenty years ago, Danny had *schlepped* two or three large bottles home in his luggage.

I have never been overly-comfortable in big social gatherings and find them even more arduous now. I hate it when I attend a *Bar-* or *Bat Mitzvah* and everyone wishes everybody else *mazeltov*. Please! Do not wish me *mazeltov*. Don't you understand? I am not celebrating anything, quite the opposite. My son will not be at his daughter's *Bat Mitzvah*.

I am no better at weddings and have not been to any since Danny died. Danny was so over-the-moon proud to be a husband and father. Although I am happy for other young, excited couples as they start their journey into marriage and eventually parenthood, I feel sorrow and anguish as I contemplate what Danny is no longer a part of. I do, however, manage to go to the *chuppah* nowadays.

DEALING WITH IT YOUR WAY

As impossible as it may seem initially, you will survive. No, you will never 'get over' the death of your child, but you will learn to move forward with your grief, to live with your loss and eventually lead a normal life again.

Socialising – your friendships change. We avoid some, some avoid us. We don't always feel like talking and sometimes others don't know what to say.

When you are ready you will want to resume socialising at a level which suits you. Friends are important, both the old ones who supported you and your new ones.

Reading – I used to be an avid reader. After Danny died, for a few years I could only concentrate long enough to read magazines. Now I prefer to read books that I find enjoyable right from the start. I do not want to endure ten to twenty hours of reading, waiting for something good to happen. I cannot read thrillers or books where a child goes missing. I want the whole experience to be a happy one.

On a different note, I received a very encouraging letter from one of the rabbis whom I approached asking for their opinions about my plan to write this book. The response was deeply heartfelt and very encouraging. For weeks I left it on my kitchen table, face up, in the irrational thinking that my darling Danny would have a chance to read it!

DOES TIME HEAL?

The biggest fallacy that gets handed around is that 'time heals'. Time does not heal – you learn to live with your pain. One of the worst pressures I felt was thinking that by a certain date I would be – should be – healed. Time lessens the sting, but for the griever, you just have to get up each morning and hope something gives you enough of a glimmer to get you through the day. Slowly you will begin to see more light. You will learn to cope.

I know of a young man who had a massive stroke. He was not expected to survive. This man spends about ten hours a day pushing himself further and further. He still has some deficits but to go see him, talk to him and realise how far he has come and that he is still working endlessly to rehabilitate himself is impressive. He has fought a mighty battle to re-enter the world. It certainly was not easy. We too must at some stage, limp back into society. The world has gone on, life has gone on – and so must we.

No one knows in advance when, or how long it will take. For us, the first year was a total write off. It seemed like my husband, Peter, was in *shule* all day long. I don't think his grief process really started until after that year – he was not in denial, but too overcome to think at all.

We heal at different rates, though we never fully heal. We become a changed person, weaker in some parts, stronger in other parts.

Just months after Danny died my daughter, while dealing with a two-year old, had a newborn who seemed to cry all the time. Meanwhile my daughter-in-law was coping on her own with her eighteen-month-old toddler. I wonder if either of these young women allowed themselves to grieve properly.

I was extremely shy for most of my younger life. I suffered from panic attacks for twelve years until Danny was diagnosed, then I had to put his pressing needs before my anxieties (and boy, that was hard). Now I am leading a support group, giving the occasional speech and speaking to all with confidence and assertion. I hate to say that Danny's death gave me this confidence, but it has spurred me forward. I feel I have taken on this role because of Danny. This gives me the impetus, the need, the urgency to reach out to other bereaved parents and offer them support – support I could have benefitted from when I needed it most.

CAN I EVER SMILE AGAIN?

Some experts say to allow one to two years to get to the point where grief is no longer the centre of your awareness. It may then take even more time to feel you have gained some semblance of your life as it was before your child died.

Initially, there was a feeling of 'How can I laugh? How can I be happy now that Danny has died?' I certainly did not want anybody to see me smiling!

Over time you will come to realise that seeking happiness does not diminish your love for your child, that the two can and should co-exist. Give yourself permission to experience happiness again. You may also grow to believe you owe it to your child to make the most of each and every day. If not, it is not only your child who has died, but you as well.

Danny was always smiling and had a delightful sense of humour (which he inherited from his mother, of course). He just made people smile. His effervescence and love of life were contagious. As a teenager he teased his older sister, convincing her that Big Ben was being sold to Italy, or that the Statue of Liberty had to be returned to France.

When diagnosed with cancer he told me that he did not want to be known as 'the kid with cancer', but as the 'cheeky bugger' (his words, not mine) that he always was.

When he died I was amazed at the number of condolences we received from people saying they would miss Danny's cheeky smile. Danny had managed to seduce his fellow solicitors and barristers with the same delightful *joie de vivre* he had as a youngster, despite having an expiry date on his life and being in constant pain.

If Danny could keep a smile on his face, surely I owe it to him to do the same.

It is ok to laugh, even though your child has died. Indeed, laughter is the best medicine. Do not be afraid to indulge. You can laugh and still love and miss your child.

By the time this book is completed, I will probably have celebrated the *Bar/Bat Mitzvah* of some of my grandchildren. I imagine I will cope. But it will bring back memories of Danny's *Bar Mitzvah*. There was great joy. There was great *naches*. Now I will be very much aware of Danny's absence, knowing he will not be a proud parent at his daughter's *simchas*.

But I know I must honour the past and embrace the future.

IT IS NOT A LOSS, IT IS A DEATH!

Some bereaved parents are offended if someone asks about the child they 'lost'. You may agonise over the semantics, that you could lose your car keys, your glasses of your wallet. You emphasize that your child died. But to be literal, you might 'misplace' any of those possessions and then find them. They are not gone forever whereas sadly, our beloved children will never return. With the death of our children we have indeed suffered a tremendous loss.

The same can be said when one asks about the child who 'passed away'. Sure, it is a euphemism, but the other person was simply being polite and offering consolation or support.

Do not be offended. Do not get caught up with trivialities.

THE DREADED QUESTION – HOW MANY CHILDREN DO YOU HAVE?

Everyone develops their own response to this. I often try to sidetrack answering by saying, 'I've got a daughter and a son and five grandchildren' and hope that puts an end to the query or turns the conversation to grandkids.

A while back I was sitting at a *Shabbat* table next to a seventeen-year-old girl, who mentioned she wanted to get into law at university. My automatic response was 'my two kids studied law'. I kicked myself as I realised, and waited for her obvious response, 'Oh really, what are they doing now?'

You're obviously not going to confide in everyone and certainly not at first meeting. I remember a conversation with a new hairdresser who asked me how many kids I have. I simply said two. She then asked where they lived. I said one here and one in Perth. And the questions continued, 'What does your child in Perth do? Married? Any kids?' I didn't go back to that hairdresser!

If you do tell people the truth, you can be faced with well-intended but inane comments like, 'I know it's not the same, but my great-uncle George/1st grade teacher/beloved rabbit died last year. He really meant a lot to me.'

It is hard to respond to such a comment, but the person is trying their best to offer comfort and are not deliberately trying to offend. And they don't expect an answer from you anyway.

Or you can get the response, 'Oh you poor thing, how did he die?' This can be particularly uncomfortable if your child took their own life. I know one lady who responds, 'He died at night-time.'

Before Danny's death I had never been irked when filling out certain health forms – 'How many children do you have?' I don't think men have to this answer this question.

YOU ARE A DIFFERENT PERSON NOW

Who would have ever imagined that you would outlive your child? You have been struck an enormous blow and your naivety has been shattered.

You may become more protective and anxious over your loved ones. You no longer take things for granted. Terrible, unimaginable things can happen, so you strengthen your resolve. You discover a new strength.

You may find that you are no longer afraid to try new things. You may enjoy meeting new people, people with whom you have a clean slate.

You are different on the inside even though you look the same. Danny broke his collar bone before birth and it had strengthened by the time he was born. Through adversity, you also have the potential to become stronger. The worst is behind you.

Different priorities

Of course, the most important priority for you is the safety of your loved ones. You realise just how precious they are.

You may no longer have time for some of your previous friends whose values are different from yours.

I am more patient and tolerant in general, although intolerant of those who do not appreciate their children.

You may develop a deeper appreciation for those who went out of their way to comfort and support you in your time of need. This may translate into you becoming more caring and compassionate to others. Life is short – for our beloved children this was especially true. So now may be the time for you to reach out, extend yourself and take on new challenges.

Memory loss and concentration

My life changed in 1999 when Danny was diagnosed with terminal cancer and I do not think my brain has been as sharp since. For many years I forced myself not to think, knowing exactly where my thoughts would lead me.

Admittedly, I am older now, but I realise that my brain is not as sharp as it used to be, and I certainly do not remember as well as I did before.

When a friend tells me they are going overseas the next day, my first thought is that they never told me they were going anywhere. Several years ago I would have claimed they forgot to tell me. Now I realise that I am sure they did, and I have forgotten.

My doctor tells me that it is not a matter of forgetting, rather not registering – you know, in one ear and out the other!

I have started doing brain-training exercises on my computer. I am getting much better. I no longer go to the wrong school to pick up the grandchildren and I manage to keep my appointments– providing I write the time down!

Altered emotions

Emotional changes may be more common in women than in men. I know I get more emotional than before. I avoid books or films that contain not only death scenes, but also any violence or aggression.

I am much more emotional than before. If I see someone crying, I am likely to join in too.

I have much more sympathy now for those who are suffering, but little patience for those malingering and always trying to pull others down to their depressed state.

Despite writing this book about the death of my child I cannot deal with other things relating to death. I am an avid crossword fan, but I cannot fill in the answers to a crossword puzzle that mention death or burial.

AFRAID YOU WILL FORGET THINGS ABOUT YOUR LOVED ONE

Accepting the death of your child does not mean you are forgetting them. Once we start to accept we can reflect on the happy times we had with our child, remember, rejoice and appreciate the joy they brought to our lives.

Danny is still a part of my life. He is not here physically but he is in other ways. I guess because he is a part of me forever. So how could I ever forget things about him?

Sure, the little things! I can't remember who his Grade 1 teacher was, or if he preferred peanut butter or vegemite on his toast, but I've forgotten that about my daughter too!

In time you may even find that the very 'grief triggers' that once caused you sadness now fill you with a sense of love and remembrance.

Recently I passed a second-hand shop and saw some car memorabilia – number plates, car badges, speedometers, etc – things that Danny loved to collect. I stood and wondered what to get for his collection before remembering Danny is no longer here.

At a much earlier stage in my journey through grief this would have been a trigger to leave me in tears, but now it's a happy memory of something about Danny.

I know a lady who, on any given day, will tell you it is so many years, months and days since her son died. Gosh! Most days I cannot even tell you what the date is, let alone do this calculation! But I know I can remember my son and when he died, without actually doing the maths.

A child is a living extension of us, so the loss feels like an amputation, just as for those who have a surgical amputation and still feel as if the limb is still attached. I feel Danny's presence constantly.

I remember Danny's generosity, his consideration, sense of humour, power of persuasion, commitment – and so much more. These are all ongoing memories of Danny in which I revel.

My memories of Danny are impossible to forget. He is a part of me and always will be, wherever he is.

Death leaves a heartache no one can heal.
Love leaves a memory no one can steal.

DO NOT RE-INVENT YOUR CHILD

We all know that you should not speak badly of the deceased but do try to remember your child honestly.

I could fill this book about Danny's virtues, but I also remember his lack of prowess on the sports field, the fruit that stayed in his school bag from Monday to Friday, his indecipherable handwriting (he inherited that from his father) and his early unwillingness to learn to read. I could go on – but you get the idea.

Do not exaggerate the virtues of your child. Otherwise you will not remember who he really was.

It is also important that you do not place your child on a pedestal as an intended source of encouragement to your other children, or compare your other children and their abilities, or lack thereof, to their deceased sibling.

BIRTHDAYS, *YAHRZEITS* AND HOLIDAYS

Throughout the year I am relatively fine, but as August comes to a close I dread turning the page of the calendar. Everyone is talking about *Rosh Hashanah*. I do not need to check the calendar to be reminded that Danny's *Yahrzeit* is a week beforehand and Danny's birthday is on 6 September. Although we don't observe it, the English date of his death is 22 September. I really wish we could skip September completely.

Your child's favourite holiday celebration may have been the family gathering for *Pesach seder*, watching the Grand Final or building a *succah* together.

One of my nephews always made a family barbecue on Boxing Day. A seat at the table will be empty now and there will be one less pair of hands to help with preparations, one less person to plan the festivities.

Many of your family holidays will be different now. You may choose to eliminate or alter the way your family commemorates certain festivals or special occasions, at least for the time being. You may, consciously or otherwise, seek to create new traditions related to a certain occasion. But I must admit that I know running away or attempting to ignore a calendar date doesn't work, so you might as well brace yourself and face each of these realities head-on.

You may find comfort in doing something special on your child's birthday, *Yahrzeit* or any other significant day. Advance planning on how to cope on these special days may help alleviate pain and reduce anxiety. Having people you love around you and sharing memories can help. In any event, many people find that anticipation prior to the day is often more difficult than the day itself.

GET INVOLVED

Your life has changed irrevocably. Whether your child was a youngster who needed you twenty-four hours a day or a young adult you only spoke to once a week, you are a different person now with different priorities, different needs and different interests.

Try something new. Express yourself in a manner you never have before. Expel those pent-up emotions through art, music, writing, exercises, hiking or drama. Both physical and creative activities are helpful.

New clubs, different people

There is comfort in anonymity. You are an explorer carving out a new world for yourself. There are no negatives here, only the potential to save yourself from depression and isolation.

Learn something new or revisit an old interest. After all, there is no need to fear failure. What is failure compared to what you have experienced? Go ahead and give it a try.

I was told that Bayside U3A was good but most of their courses were a bit too far from home. One of the few courses nearby was a philosophy course, something I had never studied and, quite frankly, did not really know what it was.

I loved the course and thrived through it. Mid-way through the second year our leader advised that he would be away for three weeks, then jokingly remarked 'unless someone else wants to take the class.' To my utter amazement, my hand went up. Remember, I was the shy kid on the block and the one who had panic attacks as a mature-aged adult.

I have made some close friends from these classes. What surprises me in listening to these new friends is that they have also had their share of misfortune.

Exercise

We all know exercise is good for us. Other than the physical benefits, exercise releases feel-good endorphins, a natural cannabis-like brain chemical and other brain chemicals. It also provides a distraction which allows us to escape the cycle of negative thoughts that feed depression.

Meditation/mindfulness

Research shows that the practice of meditation and mindfulness changes our brains and our lives, reduces anxiety and stress, boosts the immune system and increases concentration, among its many other benefits.

In addition, the practice of meditation and mindfulness can help us in healing our grief because it helps us live in the present moment, where our grief resides. It gives us better access to the 'now' thereby helping us become more aware of our pain and sadness and in turn, helping us to cope with it. Distracting ourselves from our grief is necessary and helpful from time to time, while repeatedly avoiding pain and grief only serves to prolong the journey to healing.

There are many ways to practice meditation and mindfulness. Mindfulness is a form of meditation where you are simply aware of the present moment for a short period of time – even a few minutes will do for a start. This sounds trivial except for the annoying fact that so often our mind diverts and once again we become engrossed in other thoughts.

Several years ago I was led through an experiment. The leader gave each of us one sultana and told us to put it in our mouth and think of nothing but that sultana for five minutes – its shape, size, texture, flavour and so on. Try it. Put a timer on – you cannot be watching the clock. Experience the sensation of calmness afterwards.

Meditation is the formal practice of finding peace within. Awareness of peace is achieved when mental chatter is decreased.

There are lots of mindfulness and meditation exercises on the internet or on CDs and DVDs. Whenever I cannot sleep, I play one or go through the routine from memory – I always doze off before the end.

MAKING NEW TRADITIONS

Every *Shabbat* I light a candle for Danny. I searched until I found a candleholder that I think is special.

Some people put on a *kiddush* in memory of their loved one each *Yahrzeit*, while others prefer to mourn in private.

Danny was very much into studying and furthering his knowledge of Judaism, so on his *Yahrzeit* we find it appropriate to host a *leil limmud* (night of learning) each year, which consists of a relevant *shiur* (learning session) followed by light refreshments. Only family and friends are invited.

I get too sad if I dwell on Danny's birthday. The day before it I know Danny is, or would be say, thirty-eight years old. The day after it's thirty-nine. But I do not like to think of the actual day. I know I will have trouble in 2019 when Danny would have turned forty.

This will bring back painful memories of Danny's previous 'significant birthday,' what would have been his thirtieth in 2009 – which turned out to be the day of his first *Yahrzeit.*

My daughter-in-law has instilled a beautiful tradition for my darling granddaughter, Noa, to commemorate and celebrate her *Abba's* birthday. On the day Noa gets to indulge in chips and ice-cream – *Abba's* favourite foods.

Explore ways that are meaningful to you and provide some comfort. It can include listening to your child's favourite music, writing a poem to express your thoughts, visiting a zoo or other favourite venue of your child. Alternatively, it could be making a donation, in time or money, to a special cause.

Make this tradition an opportunity to shed some grief, but also a time to remember.

LEARN TO RECOGNISE TRIGGERS

All the *Yomtovim* you celebrated with your child are going to bring back memories of previous times. As hard as it may be, try to recall the happy moments you shared.

Danny was twenty-nine, *Bar Mitzvahed*, graduated, married and a father. He had reached these coming-of-age milestones. I feel for those whose child died earlier – to watch their child's peers graduate, start dating, become young adults. Emotions are also likely to surge when you receive an invitation to a *Bar* or *Bat Mitzvah*, a wedding, or a graduation of your friends' children.

It does pain me to see Danny's classmates, accomplished professionals, proud husbands and fathers of three or four youngsters. I would like to stay in touch. I know some bereaved parents who do stay involved with their child's friends, but I admit I find it difficult although I do appreciate the efforts of a few who go out of their way with their persistence and consideration.

We have to try to share the joy for our friends whose children are having *simchas* – their life's experiences too. Seeing someone completing a life-cycle event or achieving a goal that your child will never reach, can be extremely upsetting. You may care a lot about the person celebrating – enough, sometimes, that you may be willing to play the martyr and attend. Declining invitations is often risky and may be misinterpreted, but your primary consideration should be your own feelings. If you are not up to it, tell the host so. A true friend or compassionate relative will understand. As I write this I am reminded of two individuals who both questioned 'Aren't you over Danny's death?' when I declined their invitations.

I feel for those who have younger children who approach and surpass the age at which their beloved child died. How hard that must be. Yet we cannot deprive these siblings of the joys of growing up. We must revel in their accomplishments, just as we did for their brother or sister.

What do I avoid?

I won't go to a movie or read a book if I know there is a death of a child. I opted out of my book club because I cannot read thrillers or any sad stories and I was uncomfortable when the group discussed them.

It was several years after Danny's death before I felt capable of going to the pictures and then I made sure I knew what the movie was about.

I can watch medical shows on TV, but I cannot watch a movie when a child is injured.

I love crossword puzzles – the thrill of getting one finished. But if there are any words relating to death and burial I can't pencil them in. So, you can imagine how hard it is for me writing this book!

It seemed that in the first several years after Danny's death so many of my friends had children getting married. I can go to a *chuppah* now, but my friends know and understand that I do not join in the party.

I have never been a great party-goer. I avoid most big parties especially when I am likely to bump into many old acquaintances. I am not comfortable with these people I knew twenty, thirty or forty years ago, parents of Danny's school mates or mums from the playgroups I attended, who feel they can rekindle a relationship where we left off, totally skipping over the fact of Danny's death.

I must admit, I also avoid going to *shule* except for *simchas*. It causes me immense distress. I think if Danny had died suddenly and unexpectedly I might feel differently, but having prayed for his survival for ten years I feel G-d did not listen to my prayers. Whenever I do go to *shule* I just feel out of place and have a sense of disappointment and anger. It was too early for Danny to die. I need someone to be blame and to be angry at, and for me, it is G-d.

I am not a big Facebook user and at last count I think I have eleven friends. I find it depressing when certain people post little grief 'postcards' every other day. I don't mind seeing one every now and again, but I was finding this too confronting. I have 'defriended' these individuals.

MY FUNNY LITTLE QUIRKS

It is probably a weird thing to admit, but throughout the week of *shiva* I scrawled Danny's name down the length of my thigh in thick permanent marker. In some way, I just wanted him to be 'with me' still – a bit bizarre when I am attending a *minyan* for him.

I like to wear blue as often as possible because blue was Danny's favourite colour.

I wear two ordinary rope bracelets. The blue one represents Danny's life and the black is in commemoration of his death. Certainly nothing too fancy – I don't want anyone complimenting me on my personal symbolic bracelets and telling me how pretty they look. Yes, my grief is private, but somehow, I feel the need to symbolise it. Danny's death is an integral part of me, just as his life was.

Some people may mock me and question; 'Do I really need this so that I don't forget Danny?' That's not the point. I just want him with me in any way possible. In any way I can. It is not to be reminded, it is just wanting him in my life, in me, with me, somehow.

Jewish laws prohibit tattoos and I would not normally consider it – but I would love to get one. When I mentioned this to a friend she said, 'Oooh that would hurt.' As if the pain is not there already!

When Danny needed radiotherapy, he refused a tiny pinprick of a tattoo as a marker, because it is forbidden in Jewish law. In respect of Danny's level of observance, I will never get one.

But every summer there is an outdoor market in St Kilda and I get a beautiful henna design drawn on my shoulder with Danny's name inside a heart. You don't want to know me for a while – I don't wash that shoulder until the image wears off!

After reading the draft of this book, one mother confided in me a secret only shared within her immediate family and closest friend. Ten years after the death of her child, after many years of deliberation – she got a small tattoo (in a discreet location) in memory of her child.

One bereaved mother asked me if I thought it was acceptable to burn a candle all day every day, in honour of her son. I told her that whatever she chooses to do, she does not need mine or anyone else's approval. She should do whatever she feels comfortable with, whatever gives her some moments of solace. But then she mentioned her recurring distress each time the candle in memory of her son, 'died.' I suggested she might be better off buying a small electrical *Yahrzeit* light that can stay on permanently.

I have photos of Danny all over my house, many upstairs where others do not see them. I like to look at them, to see Danny wherever I turn. I have his picture on a mug, on my keyring and in my wallet.

TALKING ABOUT YOUR CHILD

Just a few generations ago, people did not talk about the deceased. Maybe it was because deaths were more common then. Maybe they didn't know better.

I have spoken to, or tried to speak to, several people who will not talk about their deceased child. It upsets them too much.

I met a lady recently whose son died seven years ago, but she wouldn't say anymore. She refused to talk about him because it upset her too much. I respect her choice but to my mind she has buried the memories of her child together with his body. It is as if that child never existed. How sad. I thrive on my memories of Danny.

I love to talk about Danny, share his past antics and celebrate the man we loved. By a bizarre coincidence, on the eve on my wedding anniversary this year I came across an amusing so-called 'Press Release' that my darling Danny wrote in 1996, in celebration of our anniversary at that time. It displayed his usual cheeky humour. I sent a copy to my friends, both old and new, with the comment that those who knew Danny will recognise his sense of humour and those who never knew him can see what they missed out on. How could I not share that!

Talking about Danny does not cause me pain and does not deny his death. It acknowledges that he lived and keeps his memory alive.

Who and when to tell

Do talk about your child. You are his parent and he will always be a part of you. It is said that talking is therapeutic – for me there has never been any need or reason not to talk about Danny. He is and will always be my son.

We talk about Danny all the time. I feel comfortable talking about him. All my friends are ok with this and we talk about Danny or my daughter Renée, or their children – however the conversation goes.

However, I think at times some new acquaintances might find it awkward. There might be some off-handed comment – they could be talking about their child playing basketball and I will mention that Danny was a basketball referee for some years – and I get an uncomfortable look. I generally choose to ignore it and carry on.

I am as entitled to talk about all my children as much as anyone else. Some people may be uncomfortable mentioning your child's name. Tell them that you want them to, that you want to talk about your child.

However, if a new acquaintance does not know about your child it is not something you usually blurt out at your first meeting. If it is a social acquaintance, then usually conversation will soon lean towards family and you have your chance.

If it is a work-mate it may be hard to find an appropriate time. When my daughter Renée was a teenager she met a boy she liked – let us call him Jacob. On their fourth get-together he said he had something he had to tell her. He told her about his younger brother who died some years back. This was not something he was going to relate on their first meeting. Fast-forward some twenty years. Renée had been working with a small group of peers and developed a friendship with one in particular. She related to me, 'I have been working with Julie for eight months now, five days a week, we have become friends, talked about many things and I have never yet mentioned Danny's death. I feel I have to, but do not quite know how to bring it up. Now I know how Jacob felt all those years ago.'

YOUR CHILD'S POSSESSIONS, REMINDERS

Danny was not living at home when he died, so the only things in my house that belonged to him was the rubbish that he left behind and a few childish relics, like the poster from Sovereign Hill for the capture of bushranger-on-the-run, Daniel J Pollak!

It would be a painful task if your child was still living at home and everything that belonged to them was still in their cupboards and drawers, on their desk and around the house. What do you do with it all, and when? This is a very personal decision for you to make.

Some people find some comfort in wearing their adult child's favourite jumpers, jacket or Collingwood tie! Some leave their child's room and all the possessions untouched. That is their prerogative. Some people, in time, donate things to appropriate charities.

What if there are younger siblings who would grow into their older brother or sister's clothing in time? I imagine it would be very hard but also very special and reverent to see your child's possessions being worn with love and pride.

What if it is all too hard to bear? Going past your child's room, seeing the empty bed, toys and pencils all around? Some people choose to move to a new house. It is definitely advisable to delay making any major decisions in the first twelve months. Thereafter, it may be what you and your family need to do.

THE POSITIVES IN YOUR LIFE

Count your blessings. Cherish what you have. Be careful not to neglect those important to you. Personally, I am lucky Danny had twenty-nine years to show the world who he was. In the collection of inspirational writings later in this book, I relate a story about a young man I worked with, whose eight-month-old son died. Months later I was still offering my condolences and he said smilingly that those eight months were the very best in all his life.

For those with younger children who died, cherish their youthfulness, their innocence – whether they were here for 365 days, or 710, or 3,650 days, cherish every one of those days that your darling child brought joy to you and your family.

Look around you. Regardless of what year you are reading this book, I am sure there are wars, famine, rampages and attacks going on, some close to home.

Look at the people in the street. Some may be blind or deaf, without a limb or disfigured. Most have a sad story to tell.

Is your glass half full or half empty? You decide. You decide how you want to live your life. The best way to honour your child's death is to live your live as best as you can.

<u>MEMORIES</u>

The only truly dead are those who have been forgotten – a Jewish proverb

In the early weeks and months of your loss you may fear that you will forget your child, the details of the face, the tone of the voice, the special way they walked. Rest assured that while time may blur some of your memories, as you slowly shift your relationship from one of presence to one of memory, you will indeed remember.

The thoughts and memories you associate with your deceased child will never be lost – they will always be a part of you. My memories of Danny are impossible for me to forget. He is a part of me and always will be, wherever he is. I do have angry moments about Danny's death, but my memory of him does not bring tears – instead it puts a big smile on my face.

Some time ago my then four-year-old grandson went to the Traffic School for his birthday. It was a sad, but also happy memory, to show him a photo of his mother and uncle (my daughter Renée and my son Danny) when Danny also had his party at the Traffic School.

Do things that remind you of your child. My husband, Peter, never used to watch comedies but now I often find him watching Seinfeld, Fawlty Towers and MASH – Some of Danny's favourites. He hasn't quite come around to Simpsons and Family Guy yet.

If your child died from suicide, drug abuse or a protracted illness, then your more recent memories may be of tough times. Think back to happier images. I am sure there are lots of them.

MEMENTOS

Grieving parents are often comforted by physical objects associated with their child. This is not morbid or wrong. For those of us whose parents have died, I am sure we cherish various keepsakes from them, many with emotional rather than material value. In my wardrobe hangs a beautiful cable-knit jumper my mum knitted for herself. It doesn't fit me, but I get a warm feeling whenever I look at it. This is no different. It is probable that you have some awards your child received, or craft work they made in years gone by which now take on a special meaning – the *challah* cover, model car, bangle or painted masterpiece.

Some items will have a special significance and you will want to keep them forever. It is always a happy/sad memory for me, remembering twenty-nine-year-old Danny with the *Haggadah* bookmark he made in Prep!

I look at the fake faded newspaper cutting I had printed when Danny was in his teens 'Pollak to captain Australia in the One Day International' and I smile. I see the map of the world on the wall in his bedroom, with markings of the countries he visited, and I have a silent laugh when I recall the stories of his travels.

No. I am never going to forget Danny.

PICTURES

I think my love of photos started when my two children were born. By the time they were teenagers, I had over a dozen albums. When Danny was diagnosed, just days after Mum died, I spent a week at a retreat where I was introduced to the art of scrapbooking. This new hobby provided me with an excuse to take as many photos of Danny as I could over the next ten years. I get a great deal of pleasure looking through my scrapbooks, and I have many other framed photos all over the house.

I introduced one of the ladies in our group to scrapbooking. She was reluctant at first, scared to look through all her photos for fear it would upset her too much. Once she started, she was delighted to relive the happy memories. Together we made beautiful display pages of her son, from infancy through to marriage and fun times with his family. His wife and children had never seen some of the earlier photos.

We have also made framed feature pages – just one photo beautifully presented.

I have a collage of photos of Danny on one of my walls – photos from his whole life. I also have an amazing 'photo mosaic' of Danny which Renée made. From afar it is one of our favourite pictures of Danny, but if you look closer you can see it is made up of over 1000 photos.

WRITE IT DOWN

Scared you will forget little anecdotes about your child? Write them down. Ask family and friends to send you their stories. Add to them whenever you think of something else. No one else needs to ever see this. It is your private journal.

Maybe you feel inspired to write. It could be about your child, about nature or about how you feel. It is said to be cathartic to release your emotions. You might feel the need to write to your child – just go ahead.

POETRY

Poetry is not my thing. To my way of thinking every line should have the same number of syllables and every pair or alternate lines should rhyme. However sometimes that's not the case. Maybe there simply are no rules. Give it a go – you might surprise yourself.

As I am writing this I thought of my good friend Helen, for whom poetry is a life-saver. Whenever she is stressed she writes poem after poem.

I rang Helen and offered her a challenge, to write a poem about Danny within one hour. She rang me back thirty minutes later and here is what she wrote;

Danny

As a child
he was curious and cheeky.

As an adult
wise yet young at heart.

His gift was to impart
his love, knowledge and passion

in Danny fashion
to his beloved family, friends and community.

He took every opportunity
to make the most of each day.

Danny packed 129 years into his 29
leaving a legacy akin to fine wine.

Never to be forgotten,
an eternal light,
Danny

'ROOTS' PROJECT

Many children nowadays have to do a 'Roots' project at school, tracing their ancestry, learning and discovering the history of their families.

My grandchildren will have it easy because I have already completed the Pollak/Morris (my family) half of it, in scrapbook form.

My initial purpose was for Danny's daughter, my granddaughter, Noa, to have a written record of her *Abba's* family. But as I progressed and uncovered birth certificates, wedding certificates, passports, concentration camp records and army records, the significance of my project grew.

I have created a beautiful document, a timeline which led to the creation of my beautiful children and grandchildren.

PLANT A TREE

How appropriate that this should follow the Roots section! So perhaps this is also a good place to emphasise the importance of maintaining (or developing) a sense of humour.

Some parents, particularly those with a green thumb, may decide to plant a significant tree in memory of their child, or grow their child's favourite flowers, or have those flowers in the house all the time.

You might find a picture of a tree like one your child liked to climb, or a field of daisies where you sat and made daisy chains together, or a bowl of fresh berries which reminds you of those strawberry-picking expeditions.

Bring nature into your home. It may help to influence your mood.

<u>WHAT'S NEXT?</u>

"There are no goodbyes for us. Wherever you are, you will always be in my heart."
– Gandhi

FINDING A WAY TO HONOUR YOUR CHILD'S LIFE

There is a saying, 'Honour the dead by living your life.' What did your child love in life? How can you nurture that love in a positive and meaningful way?

It is wonderful if you can afford to immortalise your child in some material way – a big donation to charity, a classroom, a *Torah* or a scholarship. But you don't need to spend a lot of money to remember your child, to acknowledge them and honour their memory.

I started the Jewish Bereaved Parents support group because of Danny. It doesn't need to be in his name. Just do something in honour of your child. You will find your own strength – whether it is a special interest in the grandchildren's activities, making or delivering meals for the poor or visiting a sick neighbour.

Your life will never be the same, but with time and support you will find ways to honour your child's life while rebuilding your own.

VOLUNTEERING

If someone had suggested volunteering to me some time ago I might have sneered at them and responded that I have enough trouble dealing with myself, let alone other people. Yet since 2011, without realising it, I have been actively helping others.

Watching a group of people I brought together chat and laugh, play Scrabble or paint a picture, gives me great satisfaction.

There is so much pleasure to be had when a dozen of us spend afternoons and evenings assembling hundreds of gifts for charity, packing toys for sick kids or making bags of goodies for mums in hospital.

But the real pleasure for me is seeing the satisfaction everyone earns from what they are doing, how much benefit there is in thinking about other people who are suffering and not just ourselves.

Every single one of us now has a hole in our hearts – and in our way of life. Let's try to find useful ways to fill that void. Reach out to others in need. There are plenty of opportunities to help others, but the reward is the impact it will have on your own life.

A COLLECTION OF INSPIRATIONAL WRITINGS

BEING BEREAVED

Cynthia Pollak

This is an extract from my speech at the Australian Jewish Psychologists' Forum in October 2012, titled: 'When a Jewish child dies – helping families cope after the death of a child'.

I cannot tell you how it feels when your child dies. I cannot, because there are no words to describe it. No, there are words: anger, denial, fear, despair and guilt, but they are merely words. They don't in any way relate to the depth of pain you feel when your child dies.

Most of us in this room have had our share of misfortune. It's not a competition. I lost my parents twelve and fourteen years ago. Several years later we were robbed. Two years after that we had a fire.

I feel petty writing about all that, because it is so very insignificant compared with how it felt when, a year later our darling son, Danny, died.

All the water in the oceans, all the grains of sand on the beaches cannot compare to the magnitude of pain we felt.

For ten years Danny lived with his spreading, incurable blood-vessel cancer. Incurable, I was told, because it was so rare that research into it did not justify a share of the world's health dollar.

I had to put on a brave face for my darling son, whose life was being measured. It was hard and I sought help – until one specialist reprimanded me for 'prematurely mourning.' He spent an hour trying to give me encouragement, then shook my hand when we parted and offered me his condolences!

When Danny died my feelings were intensified, but there were two new feelings: a much greater sense of guilt and loneliness.

'G-d, out of everyone in the whole world, why pick on our son?'

Thank G-d, my brothers, my niece, nephews, cousins, friends, all my friends' children – no one – not one of them did G-d strike down.

So, what is wrong with us? What did we do wrong? Why us?

But slowly, over the weeks and months, we rationalized our guilt and saw there were others who had been dealt this same horrendous blow.

Knowing there are others does not lessen our pain and at times it can cause more anguish. But there is also a measure of comfort in having someone beside you who has been in that same hell-hole, someone who knows, who understands, who has felt that same inexplicable depth of despair you have.

What's it like being a bereaved parent? It's torture. Torture from within and way too often, from those around us.

There's the ever-dreaded first-time meet and greet question, 'How many children do you have?'

Then there are the platitudes, 'I know it's not the same, but my grandfather died last year. He really meant a lot to   me.'

I just read a book where the nine-year-old son died. A visitor commented to the mother that at least now her seven-year-old boy wouldn't be overshadowed by his brother.

I was recently invited to the engagement of a friend's daughter and explained, 'Thanks, but we don't go to engagements.' To see the young, happy, couple vowing love forever more, it's too painful. The response was, 'What? Still? But it's been four years already since your son died. Aren't you over it yet?'

No! I haven't got over my son's death and I doubt I ever will. And I will forever and ever shed a silent tear every time I hear my beautiful granddaughter calling another man 'Daddy'.

I try to avoid social functions, but recently I had to attend a Bat Mitzvah. Why does everyone wish everybody else *mazeltov*? Please! Don't wish me *mazeltov*! Don't you understand? I am not celebrating anything – quite the opposite because my son will not be at his daughter's *Bat Mitzvah.*

Yet, eventually, most of us will rejoin society.

I suffered from panic attacks for fifteen years. I didn't go to restaurants, movies, my children's concerts or graduations. Then suddenly I found myself in the consulting room at Peter MacCallum Cancer Hospital, being told my son had cancer. The only treatment for these tumours was removal of the affected site. Not possible in Danny's case, because his knee, shoulder, both hips, some ribs, spine, collarbone and both lungs were already affected.

For the next ten years I prayed over every word the bevy of specialists said, praying for a glimmer of hope. My anxieties were now focused solely on Danny's health, not my own nervousness.

Standing here and making a speech is drawing me back to the reality of normal life. But it all takes time and everyone has to find their own path.

We're Jews. And we all know we sometimes do things differently. We have different times of grief and different times of joy to non-Jews.

There is a story about two men, one Christian and the other Hindu, visiting their respective mother's graves. The Christian laughed when he saw and smelt the Hindu holding a bowl of curried specialties to put by his mother's tombstone.

'You fool,' he mocked, 'when do you think your mother is going to eat that food?'

The Hindu turned to his antagonist and replied, 'At the same time as your mother smells those roses!'

Well, we just leave a stone when we visit. We are all different, but we are all the same.

We have a Chevra Kadisha, a circle of friends, but we also need to take care of those left behind.

Through my involvement with our Jewish Bereaved Parents support group, I have learnt compassion.

I feel sorry for those whose child suffered unbearable pain, for those whose child was a youngster, or died by accident; for those parents who had to decide whether to subject their child to painful drugs in the hope of another few months; for those who lost their only child.

I can't imagine how hard any of that would be.

All of us bereaved parents face a different and difficult journey for the rest of our lives.

My darling Danny was very observant. We never discussed his prognosis, but he once commented that he was not afraid of *Olam HaBa* (the after-life) and that his future was in the hands of G-d.

Personally, I am very confused as to where I stand regarding my devotion to G-d, but, I have found comfort in the thought that although Danny's physical body has departed, his soul goes on living.

There are times when I am very down. Indeed, my life has been turned upside down. But most of the time I don't look at Danny's photo and weep. I look at the many photos of him all around my home and smile. I am so very proud and privileged to have had Danny in my life. He was truly a precious gift.

I'm almost reluctant to end this speech. With so many psychologists in this room I don't know if you will tell me I spoke well or suggest a consultation!

But I will end now, with one request. Please, cherish your kids every single day.

HE IS GONE

David Harkins[41]

You can shed tears that he is gone
Or you can smile because he has lived

You can close your eyes and pray that he will come back
Or you can open your eyes and see all that he has left

Your heart can be empty because you can't see him
Or you can be full of the love that you shared

You can turn your back on tomorrow and live yesterday
Or you can be happy for tomorrow because of yesterday

You can remember him and only that he is gone
Or you can cherish his memory and let it live on

You can cry and close your mind, be empty and turn
your back
Or you can do what he would want: smile, open your
eyes, love and go on.

---

[41] Written by David Harkins in 1982, originally titled 'Remember Me'.
https://poetrypoem.com/

LIFE AFTER DEATH – THE STORY OF TWINS[42]

Y. M. Tuckachinsky

An imaginative and telling analogy that conveys hope and confidence in the afterlife, even though this hope must be refracted through the prism of death. It is the tale of twins, still in the mother's womb, awaiting birth. It was created by a contemporary Israeli rabbi, the late Y M Tuckachinsky.

Imagine twins growing peacefully in the warmth of the womb. Their mouths are closed, and they are being fed via the navel. Their lives are serene. The whole world, to these brothers, is the interior of the womb. Who could conceive of anything larger, better, more comfortable? They begin to wonder: 'We are getting lower and lower. Surely, if it continues, we will exit one day. What will happen after we exit?'

Now the first infant is a believer. He is heir to a religious tradition which tells him that there will be a 'new life' after this wet and warm existence of the womb. A strange belief, seemingly without foundation, but one to which he holds fast. The second infant is a sceptic. Mere stories do not deceive him. He believes only in that which can be demonstrated. He is enlightened and tolerates no idle

---

[42] This analogy appears in the book *The Jewish Way in Death and Mourning* by Rabbi Maurice Lamm (Jonathan David Publishers Inc, 2000). Permission to include obtained from his son, Rabbi David Lamm.

conjecture. What is not within one's experience can have no basis in one's imagination.

Says the faithful brother: 'After our 'death' here, there will be a new and great world. We will eat through the mouth! We will see great distances and we will hear through the ears on the sides of our heads. Why, our feet will be straightened! And our heads will be up and free, rather than down and boxed in!'

Replies the sceptic: 'Nonsense. You're straining your imagination again. There is no foundation for this belief. You are looking for something to calm your fear of 'death.' There is only this world. There is no world to come!'

Suddenly, the water inside the womb bursts. The womb convulses. Upheaval. Turmoil. Writhing. Everything lets loose. Then a mysterious pounding—a crushing, staccato pounding. Faster, faster, lower, lower.

The believing brother exits. Tearing himself from the womb, he falls outward. The second brother shrieks, startled by the 'accident' befallen his brother. He bewails and bemoans the tragedy—the death of a perfectly fine fellow.

'Why? Why? Why didn't he take better care? Why did he fall into that terrible abyss?'

As he thus laments, he hears a head-splitting cry and a great tumult from the black abyss, and he trembles 'Oh my! What a horrible end! As I predicted!'

Meanwhile, as the sceptic brother mourns, his 'dead' brother has been born into the new world. The head-splitting cry is a sign of health and vigour and the tumult is really a chorus of *mazeltovs* sounded by the waiting family thanking G-d for the birth of a healthy son.

As we separate and 'die' from the womb, only to be born to life, so we separate and die from our world, only to be reborn to life eternal. The exit from the womb is the birth of the body. The exit from the body is the birth of the soul. As the womb requires a gestation period of nine months, the world requires a residence of however many years. As the womb is a corridor, an anteroom preparatory to life, so our present existence is a corridor to the world beyond.

WHERE DOES THE SOUL GO WHEN YOU DIE?

Rabbi Simon Jacobson[43]

This is a much-distorted question.

The premise is false.

Imagine a discussion between a refrigerator and electricity. The refrigerator is plugged in and is cooling food.

Now suddenly, the plug is pulled and the refrigerator says to the electricity, 'Where do you go when the plug is pulled?'

Electricity says, 'What do you mean, "where did I go?" Where did you come from? You're a little box that was just created in the last century. I have been around from the beginning of time and I am everywhere. They created a box to hold me. You have contained me. You have confined me in your box and you've become a cooling agent.'

When we ask 'Where does the soul go?', it is implying that here is where it's at. Maybe it's the other way around and the soul is where it's at. And this world is a newcomer.

We're like the box, like the refrigerator. The soul enters this box for a period of time and then it just goes back to its natural place. The fact that you're not familiar with that place is like how a refrigerator is not familiar with electricity. All it is, is a box. We have very narrow vision. We don't see the larger journey of life, all the stages in the journey. It doesn't necessarily relieve the pain of loss, of

---

[43] Rabbi Simon Jacobson is head of The Meaningful Life Centre in New York. Permission to include has been obtained from him.

death. But it makes you understand that a soul does not go anywhere. It may be right here, but it is not contained in the same container any more.

WHY DO SOME OF THE BEST DIE YOUNG?

Rabbi Aron Moss[44]

A great debate once raged in heaven. It was over a most beautiful and precious new soul that G-d had created. The angels debated what should be done with this soul. One group of angels demanded that this soul remain in heaven. 'She is too pure, too holy to face the ugliness of the lowly world,' they said. 'Who knows what will happen to her in a world of temptation and evil. This soul must stay with us here.'

But the other group of angels said the exact opposite. 'Indeed, this soul glows with a unique divine glow. But for that very reason she must go down to earth. For imagine the beauty and goodness this soul can bring to a dark world. What good is there in keeping such a soul in heaven? Let her descend to earth and shine her light there.'

And so they argued back and forth, each side unshakable in their view. Until it became clear that they could not resolve the issue themselves, they needed a higher authority. The case was brought before G-d Almighty. The angels stated their arguments before the heavenly court. G-d listened to the two opinions: the first group of angels arguing that this unspoiled soul is too holy to be plunged into the lowly world, the second countering that the world needs such souls more than anything.

And this was G-d's response:

---

[44] Rabbi Aron Moss is the Rabbi of Nefesh Shul, Sydney. Permission to include has been obtained from him.

'Indeed, it is sad to send such an immaculate soul into such a dark world. But this is My will. I only created darkness so souls like this one can transform darkness into light. The whole purpose of creation was that the lowly world be refined by the good deeds of mortal human beings. This cannot be achieved by souls in heaven. It can only be achieved through souls in bodies. And so even this most perfect and pure soul must descend to earth.'

The first group of angels, who had requested the soul to remain in heaven, were disappointed. They couldn't fathom how such a spiritual being could be expected to survive such a physical world. G-d turned to them and said, 'As for your request to keep this soul up here, I will grant it partially. Though she must leave us and go down to earth, it will not be long before she will return to us. Her sojourn on earth will be brief. Such a brilliant soul will not need long to fulfil her mission. Soon she will be free to come back to heaven.'

 G- d then turned to the second group and asked, 'Are you satisfied with that? Do you accept that this soul can only be on earth for a limited time?'

The angels replied, 'Yes we do. Every day that she is on earth is a blessing.'

ʠ ʠ ʠ

When a loved one passes away we feel we have lost something precious. We are left with a gaping hole in our heart and often wonder why they were taken away from us. But at the same time we can be grateful for the very fact that they were given to us in the first place. We are blessed to have such beautiful souls in our lives. The world is privileged to have such heavenly guests come down on earth. Even if it can only be for a short while, we will take whatever we can get.

In time, all souls will be reunited. In the meantime, let us be thankful for the gift of every day.

THE GIFT

Cynthia Pollak

In the mid-1990s one of my work colleagues and his wife had their first child. Each day Philip kept us updated with baby Gabriel's progress.

One day Philip didn't come to work and we were all shocked to hear that baby Gabriel had died.

Two months later, the office was filled with Xmas cheer. Philip was back at work. I had a good working relationship with him, but I didn't want to upset him by wishing him 'Season's Greetings'. I was keenly aware of his loss.

But Philip surprised me by giving me a Xmas present! I was taken aback and embarrassed. I explained that I didn't think he would want to acknowledge Xmas this year let alone celebrate it, having recently suffered such a loss.

Philip was all the more astounded! 'Oh no', he replied, 'we were so blessed this year.   G-d gifted Gabriel to us for eight precious months.'

I have tried to have this attitude also. My dear son, Danny, died in 2008, aged twenty-nine. I mourn for him desperately, but I try to focus on the gift we all shared for those twenty-nine years.

A PERSONAL STORY

Cynthia Pollak

I want to share a little story with you.

In 2011 my husband and I went to Thailand, our first holiday since our son Danny had died three years earlier. At first, we were both fairly traumatized, especially as we had booked into five-star accommodation – which made it seem all the more wrong to be enjoying ourselves so much. We were torn with guilt!

After the first week, we moved down south. The accommodation was pathetic. I broke my toe. Now we started to relax.

I brought a present back for my friend Marina. About nine months earlier, Marina's son, Mark, had died suddenly of a previously unknown heart condition. We had been in contact for several months.

I invited Marina to meet me for coffee. As I gave her the present I told her that after Danny died my husband Peter and I both agreed that there was no way either of us would ever want to give or receive presents any more. Material things are just useless, serve no purpose, won't bring Danny back, won't give us any joy. And we didn't, for a while: no birthdays, no Mother's Day or Father's Day presents. Yet this year, my daughter gave me an iPad for Mother's Day. I have been involved with computers since I was a teenager in the 1970s and I was rapt! A door was opened ...

So I gave Marina this little trinket. I was delighted to see how genuinely pleased she was that I had thought of her. Then I confided my past feelings.

Amid tears from both of us, Marina then told me that yesterday was her birthday, and the day before was her husband's birthday. They agreed on no presents and both spent the two days crying. Yet here she was, genuinely happy to be receiving my gift. And she said it truly did bring a touch of light back into her life.

UNDERSTANDING OUR PAIN – THE PRINCE AND THE PEASANT

Harriet Sarnoff Schiff[45]

Note from Cynthia: Several months after my son died, I read a few books, but none of them gave me any satisfaction until I was given a small book called *The Bereaved Parent*, by Harriet Sarnoff Schiff. Like many of the books I read it was written by a bereaved parent, but somehow this was the only one that 'spoke' to me from the very first chapter, with the retelling of the tale you are about to read.

For the purpose of including this story in my book, I contacted the author, and have taken the liberty of including her response here.

Dearest Cynthia,
Firstly, *Shabbat shalom*
Of course you may use any part of *The Bereaved Parent* that is useful.
I am truly sorry we share such a painful sisterhood.
I love that you are doing your work with a Jewish theme. Our faith means a great deal to me and it has helped guide me through some very dark passages.
How wise you are to take the parts of the Compassionate Friends organisation into your group that work for you and incorporate them with the parts of our Jewishness that speak to us.
My son and daughter have made it one of their life purposes to visit families who have surviving siblings, to talk with them and remind the parents how important those who are alive still are.
It gets all too easy in the miasma of pain to lose sight of this vital aspect of the process.

---

[45] From the book *The Bereaved Parent*, by Harriet Sarnoff Schiff (Penguin Books, 1978). Permission to include obtained from her.

Please let's stay in touch and thank you again for your kind words

Harriet

≈ ≈ ≈

There is a tale about a prince fleeing from revolutionaries determined to kill him and take away his throne. The prince, terrified, sought shelter in a peasant's cottage.
Although the peasant had no idea the frightened man was a member of the nobility, he gave the prince refuge by telling him to hide under the bed. The prince had no sooner done so when his pursuers battered down the door and began to search the cottage.
The revolutionaries searched everywhere. When they came to the bed they decided to prod it with knives rather than move the cumbersome piece of furniture. At last they left.
The prince, pale but alive, crawled out from under the bed after hearing the pursuers depart. He turned to the peasant then and said, 'I think you should understand that you have just saved the life of your prince. Name three favours and I will grant them.'
The peasant, a simple man, thought for a while and said,

'My cottage is in great disrepair and I have not had the money to fix it. Can this be done?'
'Fool!' cried the prince. 'Of all things in the world, why did you ask so small a favour? I will honour your wish, but what is your next request?'
'Sire, my neighbour sells the same wares as me in the market place. Would it be possible to change his location so both of us could make a better livelihood?'
'Idiot,' said the prince. 'Of course I will do as you wish. What foolishness, when you could have riches, to ask such nonsense! Take care that you do not anger me with another silly request.'

No longer able to restrain his curiosity, the peasant said, 'As my third request I ask only that you tell me how you felt as the knives were being pushed through the bed.'

The prince, infuriated, shouted, 'How dare you offend majesty by asking about my emotions? For this act I will have you beheaded tomorrow!'

The prince called in a few of his retainers and had the hapless man carried off to the local jail.

All through the night the man wept for his folly and feared what would happen on the morrow.

When the sun rose, his jailers came to him and led him into a courtyard where an executioner with his black hood stood awaiting the terrified man.

Forced to kneel on the block, he heard a soldier call, 'One, two … ' but before he could say 'three' another soldier on horseback came tearing into the courtyard calling, 'Stop! The prince commands it.'

With those words the executioner, whose blade had been resting on the peasant's neck, withdrew the sword. The shaking man arose and faced the soldier who had saved his life.

'His Highness gives you his pardon and orders me to give you this note,' said the soldier.

The peasant, relieved to the point of tears, began to read the few terse words, 'As your final favour you wanted to know how I felt under that bed when the revolutionaries came. I have granted your request because now you know!'

The prince had shown the peasant more graphically than words could possibly have done just what the horrendous ordeal had been like.

The prince, no fool, had realized that some things are beyond description. No matter how eloquent the words, their impact can fall flat when not accompanied by similar experience.

And so it is with bereaved parents.

No one has gone through this catastrophe without thinking sometime or other: 'You can't possibly know what it feels like!'
It is rare not to think this, as loving friends and family try in vain to comfort and soothe the pain. All their kindness is almost meaningless in the face of the despair a parent feels when outliving a child.
As the prince illustrated to the peasant, the emotions one feels are only believable and truly understood by a fellow bereaved parent.

THE BOOK OF LIFE

Renée Sion[46]

Danny bought me a *Rosh Hashanah machzor* in September 2001, three years after his diagnosis and seven years before he died. He inscribed it with 'The *Torah* is a tree of life to those who cling to it.' (Proverbs 3.18)

I've never before considered what this statement really meant nor why he chose to inscribe my *Rosh Hashanah machzor* with this in particular. To consider this in the context of *Rosh Hashanah*, I had to learn about exactly what *Rosh Hashanah* is.

It is during the day of *Rosh Hashanah* that *G-d* and His Heavenly Court sit in judgment on every individual. The heavenly ledgers are opened and every person's deeds are counted and scrutinised. The *Talmud* speaks of the ledgers of the living and the ledgers of the dead. But what does the *Talmud* mean when it refers to the living and the dead? And how are the ledgers actually calculated?

'Alive' is not simply alive, and 'dead' is not dead as I had always assumed was the case.

I have struggled each year on *Rosh Hashanah* to reconcile my desire to be written in what I thought was the Book of Life, when Danny had, it appeared, been written in the Book of Death.

---

[46] This is an extract from My daughter Renée's speech, at the ninth *Yartzeit* service for Danny, September 2017

What I have learnt today is that 'alive' and 'dead' carry more meaning than the dictionary definitions given by the sages. People are alive if their achievements are worthwhile and they are dead if their lives are devoid of spiritual content.

It is written in the *Talmud*: 'The righteous are considered alive even when they are dead; the wicked are considered dead even when they are alive.'

Those who live to serve *G-d* through studying the *Torah* and conducting themselves according to its laws – whether in *shule* or life or business – are recorded in the ledgers of the living, and are inscribed on *Rosh Hashanah* for the eternal life of the spirit.

Those whose lives are devoid of such content can justly be regarded as if they were dead, even though they breathe, eat and propagate. When it is clear in the judgment that someone falls into that category, he is tragically inscribed in the ledgers of the dead.

There is a third category: those who are in-between. Such people vacillate between righteousness and wickedness.

When the Day of Judgment begins, no-one is condemned to remain in the category of the wicked or the in-betweens, because this is not only the Day of Judgment but the first of the Ten Days of Repentance. For these people, the period of judgment extends until *Yom Kippur.*

I also researched about how *Hashem* performs His judgment, about how the arithmetic is done. What I learnt is that when we are judged, *Hashem*'s judgment is perfect in terms of accuracy. It is not limited to time. To Him, past, present and future are not imperative considerations.

This means that when *Hashem* sees a person, He sees everything the person has ever done, even the potential, drives, ambitions and values that will shape his future actions. Everything a person has ever done is calculated and he is judged by the quantity and quality of his deeds, his ethics, morality, intent, sincerity and so on. *Hashem* sees the total man as if he were living his whole life in that instant.

The same holds true for what he will do in the future. The person who is capable of performing greatness is not the same as someone else who will never rise above his present state of distinction or mediocrity.

It provides me with much comfort to know that Danny is/was judged according to his whole life, as if he had done everything he might have done, but for the fact that he is no longer here.

I think back to 2001 when Danny inscribed my *machzor*. I cannot remember how sick he was at the time. Yes, he had been diagnosed with incurable cancer, but I don't think death was on his mind. Nonetheless, I think he chose to inscribe my *machzor* with this statement because it symbolized his dedication to the *Torah*, and he extended it out like a branch for me to grasp.

Danny lived to serve *Hashem* through studying the *Torah*, but he wasn't just a 'student' of *Torah*, he was a 'doer'. He conducted himself according to its laws in every facet of his personal and professional life. He applied himself and developed an appreciation for the *Torah*'s wisdom. He is someone for whom the *Torah* became a Tree of Life. He directed his body as well as his soul. The *Torah* afforded him a sense of the infinite – a Tree of Life in store for the righteous in the World to Come.

I approach this *Rosh Hashanah* differently. I have learnt that the *Torah* is a Tree of Life if I choose to cling to it, the biggest reward of which is a shortcut to the ledgers of the living, which is precisely where I assume Danny's name is written.

THE SANDBOX

Anonymous[47]

This is the story of a little boy who goes out with his father. The boy sees a sandpit and goes off to play there.

He has a wonderful time, playing in the sand, making friends, chatting away, building in the sand, bulldozing his creations – all the fun of a sandpit, with his new friends.

But after a while the father says it's time to go. The young boy doesn't want to go. He even puts up a bit of a fuss. Maybe he resents his father for a while. He doesn't want to leave the sandpit, leave all the fun behind, leave his friends. But his father insists.

Of course, the boy does go with his father, back home. He trusts his father. He knows his father is right. He is his protector and has the boy's best interests at heart. Really, he is the boy's best friend for all time.

So too, it is the same when G-d calls his child to go back home — to leave his family and friends here on earth, to leave the fun times and go back.

---

[47] Text composed from what I remember from a talk several years ago. I cannot remember the speaker.

AN OLD LADY'S FUNERAL

Rabbi Tuvia Bolton[48]

In the New York home of an Orthodox Jewish family, the phone rang one evening with bad news: their ninety-year old mother, who had been in a nursing home for the aged, had passed away quietly in her sleep.

Everyone wept, funeral arrangements were made, and early the next afternoon family and friends gathered to pay their last respects.

The next few days were busy, but on the afternoon of the third day there was a strange phone call. The voice on the other end said, 'Hello! Is this Avi? Is everything all right? Are Mommy and Daddy there? What do you mean who is it? Don't you recognize your grandma? So let me talk to Mom or Dad'.

Her son got on the phone and said hesitantly, 'Mom, is this you?'

'Mom is still alive!' he said with a wild look of disbelief.

The joy was great! He told her they were on their way to visit her and in no time they were by her side explaining the whole thing. It had obviously been a terrible mistake.

But suddenly it dawned on them. They had just made a funeral and buried someone! Who was that someone? And who were her relatives?

They called the manager of the nursing home and told him. It appears that in the same building was another

---

48 Rabbi Tuvia Bolton is Rosh Yeshiva at Yeshiva Ohr Tmimim, Israel. Permission to include obtained from him.

patient with the same name as their mother. Both were Holocaust survivors, both were in their nineties and both were very similar in build. So somehow the management confused the identities, made a terrible mistake and informed the relatives of the living one instead of the deceased.

The deceased woman had only one relative, a son who lived not far away. They all agreed that it would be best if the family of the living woman deliver the bitter news. After all, they reasoned, probably the son would be angry and they could calm him down by assuring that she was given the utmost honour and respect, show him the gravesite, etc.

But they were in for a surprise. As soon as he picked up the phone and heard they were calling from the nursing home and would like to visit him he interrupted and said, 'If you're calling to say my mom died, no need to come. Just cremate her, throw away the ashes and send me the bill. Okay?'

They were shocked. But when they asked if they could come speak to him, he agreed. A half-hour later, they were sitting in his home trying to explain to him that cremation is forbidden according to Jewish law and the custom is there should be a proper Jewish burial. Moreover, there is the raising of the dead, etc.

But he wanted no part of it, on principle. Not only was cremation cheapest, most efficient, space and time-saving, it was realistic. All this business about souls, G-d, Judaism and raising of the dead was all nonsense as far as he was concerned.

Finally they had no choice but to tell him the truth. His mother had actually died several days ago. But by mistake they were told the recently deceased woman was their mother and so they not only gave her a Jewish burial, they had already sat three days of *Shiva* for her.

'What?' He held his head in his hands and whispered, 'Buried? Mom got buried?' He had this strange, stunned look on his face. He closed his eyes, his face contorted and suddenly he burst out weeping uncontrollably like a baby. From time to time he said, 'Oy! Buried!'

After ten minutes he calmed down and explained. 'My mother was a Holocaust survivor. All her family got killed by the Germans, along with my father and all his family. But she got out with me. I was just a baby then, but we moved to America and after all that happened to her, she still believed in G-d.'

'At first everything was okay, but as I got older, like fifteen or sixteen, I didn't want to be different from everyone else, so I dropped Judaism. She started bugging me about how we are different, how I should marry a Jewish girl and eat kosher food, etc., but it just made me mad.

'We used to have big arguments until I got so fed up I told her I'm not going to live a life like hers. As far as I'm concerned there is no such thing as G-d or afterlife or souls or Judaism and when I die I'm going to have my body cremated and that's what I'll do to hers also when she dies. I guess it was sort of cruel, but I thought it was for her good, that she should start living in a real world and leave the 'superstitions' behind.

'Finally I told her, "I'll make a deal." She should pray to G-d. If she's right and G-d exists, then He'll see to it that she gets a burial but if not, then cremation. I was a hundred percent sure, no doubt at all, what the outcome would be.

'Now I see I was wrong! All this time she was right! Do you understand what happened? G-d listened to her prayers! She was right!' And he began weeping anew.

On the spot he agreed to observe the seven days of mourning for her in the house of the previous 'mourners' and to begin learning about Judaism.

BE PATIENT AND HAVE FAITH IN G-D.[49]

Rabbi Elchonon Wasserman *z"l*, was a prominent rabbi and *Rosh Yeshiva* in pre-World War II Europe. He was martyred in the Kovno Ghetto. This was his response when asked by a fellow captive to explain why such bad things were befalling them.

Once there was a man who knew nothing about agriculture. He went to a farmer to learn about farming. The farmer took him to his field and asked him what he saw. He saw a beautiful piece of land full of grass and pleasing to the eye. Then the visitor stood aghast as the farmer ploughed up the grass and turned the beautiful green field into a mass of brown ditches.

'Why did you ruin the field?' asked the man.

'Be patient and you will see,' answered the farmer.

Then the farmer showed him a sack full of plump kernels of wheat and asked him what he saw. The visitor described the nutritious inviting grain and then once more watched in shock as the farmer ruined something beautiful. This time he walked up and down the furrows and dropped kernels into the open ground wherever he went; then he covered them up with clods of soil.

'Are you insane?' the man asked. 'First you destroy the field, then you take this beautiful grain and you throw it underneath.'

The farmer answered, 'Be patient and you will see.'

---

[49] This response appears on various sites on the internet. I found it on http://rabbisedley.blogspot.com.au

---

Time went by until once more the farmer took his guest out into the field. Now they saw endless straight rows and green stalks sprouting up from all of the furrows. The visitor smiled broadly, 'I apologize. Now I understand what you were doing. You made the field more beautiful than ever. The art of farming is truly marvellous.'

'No,' said the farmer, 'we are not done, you must still be patient.'

More time went by and the stalks were fully-grown. Then the farmer came with a sickle and chopped them all down as his visitor watched open-mouthed, seeing how the orderly field became an ugly scene of destruction. The farmer bound the fallen stalks into bundles and decorated the field with them. Later he took the bundles to another area, where he beat and crushed them until they became a mass of straw and loose kernels. Then he separated the kernels from the chaff and piled them up in a huge hill. Always he told his protesting visitor, 'Be patient, we are not done.'

Then the farmer came with the wagon and piled it high with grain, which he took to the mill. There this beautiful grain was ground into formless choking dust. The visitor complained again, 'You have taken beautiful grain and transformed it into dust.' Again he was told to be patient.

The farmer put the dust into sacks and took it back home. He took some dust and mixed it with water, while his guest marvelled at the foolishness of making whitish mud. Then the farmer fashioned the mud into the shape of a loaf. The visitor saw the perfectly formed loaf and smiled broadly, but his happiness did not last. The farmer lit a fire and put the loaf into the oven. 'Now I know you're insane. After all that work you burn what you make.' The farmer looked at him and laughed, 'Have I not told you to be patient?'

Finally the farmer opened the oven took out the freshly baked bread, crisp and brown, with an aroma that made the visitor's mouth water.

'Come,' the farmer said. He led his guest to the kitchen table where he cut the bread and he offered his now-pleased visitor a liberally buttered slice. 'Now,' the farmer said, 'Now you understand.'

Rav Elchonon said, '*Hashem* is the farmer and we are the fools who do not begin to understand his ways or the outcome of his plan. Only when the process is complete will all the Jewish people know why all this happened. Then, when *Moshiach* has finally come, we will know why all of this had to be. Until then we must be patient and have faith that everything, even when it seems destructive and painful, is part of the process that will produce goodness and beauty.'

EVERYTHING G-D DOES IS FOR THE GOOD

Rabbi Shlomo Majeski[50]

The *Talmud* tells us that once, while Rabbi Akiva was on a journey, he needed a place to spend the night. He knocked on the door of one of the homes in the town he was passing through, but the owner did not invite him in. He was not upset, for he realized, 'Everything G-d does is for the good.'

He knocked on another door, but again he was not offered hospitality. His reaction remained the same, 'Everything G-d does is for the good.' Even after he had gone from door to door and realized that no one in the town was going to accept him as a guest, he still said, 'Everything G-d does is for the good.'

He had no choice but to camp in a forest at the outskirts of the town. He was traveling with a donkey to carry his packages, a rooster to wake him up early and a lamp with which he could study at night. Shortly after he encamped, a lion devoured his donkey, his rooster was killed by another predator and a strong wind blew out his lamp. After each of these events, Rabbi Akiva said, 'Everything that happens is for the good.'

And the *Talmud* continues, telling us that he was right. On the following morning, he discovered that during the night a Roman legion had attacked this village and taken its people as captives. Had he been accepted as a guest in one of these homes, he too would have been taken captive.

---

[50] Rabbi Shlomo Majeski is the principal of Machon L'Yahadus, a yeshiva for women in Brooklyn. Permission to include obtained from him.

And if his donkey or rooster had been alive, their braying and crowing would have attracted the legionnaires' attention. Had his lamp remained burning, they would have been able to see him in the forest. 'Everything that happened was for the good.'

THE REINCARNATED PRINCE

Rabbi Tuvia Bolton

Some three hundred years ago, the name of Rabbi Israel Baal Shem Tov spread throughout Europe as one who was willing to do anything, even perform miracles like Elijah and Moses, in order to help another – especially a fellow Jew.

One evening a middle-aged couple came with a desperate request. They wanted a child. Despite their prayers, good deeds and various remedies and treatments, they had failed to conceive a child in all the years of their marriage.

The Baal Shem Tov closed his eyes, put his face into his hands, lowered his head to the desk before him and his consciousness soared to the spiritual realms.

Minutes later he sat upright, looked at them sadly and said, 'There is nothing I can do. Continue praying, continue your good deeds. May G-d have mercy. But it is beyond my ability to help you.'

The woman burst into bitter tears while her husband turned his face aside and wept silently, his body shaking.

'No, no!' she cried. 'I won't believe it. I will not accept no for answer. I know that when a *tzaddik* (righteous person) decrees, G-d must fulfil. I want a child!' Her cry pierced the walls and broke the holy master's heart.

He lowered his head again for many long minutes then looked up and said, 'Next year you will have a child.'

The couple was speechless. The man began trembling, took the Baal Shem Tov's hand and kissed it as his wife showered thanks and blessings. They backed out the door, bowing, weeping and praising G-d and His servant, the holy Rabbi Israel.

Sure enough, two months later the woman conceived, and nine months thereafter gave birth to a beautiful baby boy.

The couple's joy increased day by day as the child grew. Their baby was beautiful! His eyes sparkled with life and his every smile filled their lives with warmth and happiness. At the age of one year, it was obvious he was something special; he was already walking and talking. As he approached the age of two they began looking for a tutor to begin teaching him Torah. They planned to take him to the Baal Shem Tov to show him what his blessing had brought.

But on the morning of his second birthday the child didn't wake up.

The neighbours came running when they heard the screams, but nothing could be done. As miraculously as the boy had come, so mysteriously and tragically had he departed this world.

The funeral was enough to make the heavens cry. After the week of mourning they returned to the Baal Shem Tov to inform him of the tragedy. But the Baal Shem Tov understood better than they could possibly have imagined.

'Your child,' he said to the grieving parents, 'contained a lofty soul which had made a huge sacrifice to save thousands of people. But this soul needed you to achieve its *tikkun* (rectification) and become spiritually complete. That day, when you came to me, I looked into the heavens and saw that it was impossible for you to have children. But when I heard your cries and saw the depth of your pain, I realized that this special soul was destined to be yours for the short span of its return to physical life. Sit down, dear friends, I have a story to tell you.'

Several hundred years ago lived a king who was childless. He was rich and powerful, but he desperately desired a son to carry on the lineage. He ordered that all his subjects hold daily prayers in their houses of worship that G-d should grant their sovereign an heir.

One of his advisors suggested that the reason the king was childless was because his Jewish subjects did not pray for him sincerely enough. The only way to make them do that, said this advisor, was to oppress them.

The next day the king issued a public proclamation stating that if the queen was not blessed with a child within the next three months, all the Jews would be expelled from his kingdom. With all the neighbouring countries closed to Jewish settlement, the poor Jews had nowhere to go. Their cries and prayers rose from every synagogue in the land.

A call resounded through the heavens for a soul willing to descend into the spiritually desolate environment of the royal palace in order the save the Jews of that land. Finally, one very holy soul agreed to make the sacrifice.

Shortly thereafter, the queen became pregnant and soon gave birth to a son. The king was overjoyed and showered the Jews of his realm with presents and favours.

At the age of two the child could already read and write, and when he was five years old he had surpassed all his teachers. A master teacher, a priest whose fame as a genius and scholar had spread far and wide, was brought from afar to teach the prodigy.

This new tutor was of a different calibre altogether. It seemed that he had mastered every form of wisdom in the world and his very presence radiated a thirst for knowledge. The young genius could not get enough of his new teacher. He became attached to him more than even to his own father, the king. He spent every moment of the day and most of the night with him, absorbing more and more wisdom and learning; and the more he absorbed the more he desired.

But the priest demanded his times of privacy. He had an agreement with the king that for two hours every day he would lock himself in his room and no one, not even the king himself, was allowed to enter or disturb him in any way. It was on this condition that he accepted the task of teaching the prince.

But the prince was curious. He could not tolerate the idea that his beloved master was withholding something from him. He had to know everything!

One day, the young prince managed to hide himself in his teacher's room before the priest's daily two hours of seclusion. The priest entered the room, locked the door securely behind him and searched the room thoroughly. Somehow he failed to discover the prince's hiding place and proceeded in his strange daily ritual.

First he removed all the crosses from the walls and from around his neck and put them in a box outside his window. Then he took out a large white woollen shawl with strings at the corners, wrapped it completely around his head and body and began weeping like a baby.

Then he took out two small black boxes with long black straps attached to them, tied one to his left upper arm and the other above the middle of his forehead. After that he began to pray, swaying, singing and crying for over an hour. Finally, he took out a large Hebrew text and began reading from it in a sing-song voice, swaying back and forth all the time.

Suddenly, he stopped and listened intently. The faint but unmistakable sound of another person in the room had caught his ear. The priest was terrified. He jumped from his chair, hurriedly removed the black boxes and shawl, stuffed them in a drawer, and began to search the room. It did not take long for him to discover his young pupil, who had been observing everything with rapt fascination.

The priest begged the boy not to reveal what he saw. If the king found out he would certainly be beheaded. But the prince's curiosity had been aroused. He swore that he would never tell anyone what he saw in the room, but only if the priest would explain what he had just done and teach him what it was all about.

So the priest had no choice but to reveal that he was a Jew, doing what Jews have been doing for thousands of years: praying and studying the *Torah* and fulfilling its commandments. He had been compelled to hide his faith during one of the many decrees of forced conversions that Jews were subjected to in those times; now on the pain of death he was forced to assume the guise of an alien religion.

'You must teach me your ancient wisdom,' the prince insisted. 'I knew that you were hiding something from me. In everything that you taught me, I always sensed that there was something more there, something deeper and truer, that you were withholding from me!' In vain did the 'priest' plead that he would be subjecting them both to mortal danger. 'If you refuse to teach me,' the prince threatened, 'I'll tell everyone what I saw in this room.'

For several years they learned *Torah* together, until the boy announced that he wanted to convert to Judaism. His desire became so strong that teacher and pupil made up a story about going to Rome to further their studies.

Instead, they escaped to another country where the boy converted and never returned to the palace again.

'The prince became a great and famous sage,' the Baal Shem Tov concluded his story, 'living a life of saintliness and good deeds. When he passed on from this world and his soul ascended to the heavens, it was the most luminous soul that had returned from earth in many generations. Only one blemish dimmed its shining perfection – the lingering effect of the fact that it had been conceived, borne and fed for two years in the spiritually negative environment of the royal palace. All it lacked to attain the true heights of its glorious potential was for it to return to earth and be conceived, given birth to and weaned in the holy atmosphere of a righteous home.'

'When I saw the depth of your holy desire for a child, I know that you were worthy parents for this righteous soul.'

KEEPING A TRADITION

Harriet Sarnott Schiff

One family, while trying to avoid Thanksgiving, which also happened to be their deceased child's birthday that year, decided that family gatherings were no longer for them. They would travel, or simply ignore the festivities.

One day, the mother came upon her ten-year-old daughter crying and asked her what was wrong.

'She was sobbing,' reported the mother. 'All the children at school had told of their plans and made table decorations for the holiday. Linda felt completely removed from her classmates. She cried that not only was she deprived of her brother, who had died, she couldn't even have Thanksgiving dinner and a turkey.

'I listened to her, held her in my arms and cried. What she was saying made sense. After all, we still had three living children. They also mattered.

'That night I talked to my husband and we decided that no matter how bleak and empty it would be, we would have a traditional Thanksgiving dinner.'

The mother said the family sat around the table, very quietly at first. The father said grace, and thanked the Lord for a beautiful meal. When he was through, their ten-year-old said she had something to add.

'I want to thank Mommy and Daddy for making this very special dinner for our family. And most of all I want to thank you G-d for letting us have our brother Eric for six years.'

SLEEP, THE *TALMUD* TELLS US, IS ONE-SIXTIETH OF DEATH

In death the body no longer returns.

(Why I know Danny is safe – a note by Cynthia)

Is it not strange that humankind so desperately needs sleep on a regular basis? We believe that G-d created us to live lives of purpose, to fulfil divinely appointed responsibilities, accomplish significant tasks. So why did He make it necessary for us to take time out in such a consistent way, with an activity that seems to allow us to accomplish nothing? Surely He could have made our bodies function without these eight hours of total idleness out of our twenty-four hour days.

So why sleep?

The wisdom of *Kabbalah* gives us a profound answer. We sleep because G-d cannot bear to be away from us too long without closer contact.

When we sleep our souls ascend heavenward. Only a residue remains to keep our bodies alive. The rest returns to its source to be reinvigorated and refreshed with spiritual nourishment. We who are created in the image of G-d need more than the food we ingest for our bodies during the day in order to survive. The out-of-body experience we call sleep is a trip we have to make on a daily basis to keep our sanity, so that our souls do not perish of starvation from being deprived of heavenly sustenance.

Sleep, the *Talmud* tells us, is one sixtieth-of death. The similarity is based on the physical separation of the soul from the body. In death it no longer returns. In life, the soul comes back from its meeting with the divine to hopefully tackle the challenges of daily living with the insights and inspiration gained from its journey.

SEEING THE SILVER LINING

Rabbi Shlomo Majeski[51]

The *Chassidic* approach to joy

Since G-d is the epitome of goodness, everything that happens has a positive purpose. The more we understand the connection between G-d and our world – how they are really one – and the more we understand how G-d controls every event that occurs, the more we can understand how everything is ultimately good.

However, certain things happen in life that we cannot conceive of as being good. We try to adopt a new perspective, to look from this angle or from that vantage point, and still these things do not appear good. In the story of Rabbi Akiva or in the story of Nachum Ish Gamzu, it took a day or several days for everyone to see how what happened was for the good. But there are certain times when you just cannot make the connection. In fact, sometimes, we see a person perform a good deed or act pleasantly, yet a short while later, he is forced to suffer because of it.

How can this be explained? One of the classic explanations comes from the *Midrash* where it describes a journey one of the Sages, Rabbi Yehoshua ben Levi, shared with Eliyahu HaNovi, Elijah the Prophet.

Once, when Rabbi Yehoshua encountered Eliyahu HaNovi, he asked Eliyahu if he could accompany him so he could learn from his conduct. Eliyahu refused,

---

[51] Rabbi Shlomo Majeski is the principal of Machon L'Yahadus, a yeshiva for women in Brooklyn. Permission to include obtained from him.

explaining that Rabbi Yehoshua would not understand what he would see. On the contrary, his mortal mind would raise countless questions and there would be no time for explanations.

Rabbi Yehoshua ben Levi nevertheless begged and pleaded and promised he would not ask any questions. Eliyahu finally agreed on the condition that as soon as Rabbi Yehoshua began to ask questions, they would part company.

And so they set out together. Toward evening, they reached an old, shaky hut. An elderly couple was sitting outside. While their features bespoke a dimension of dignity, they were obviously poor. But their poverty did not hamper their enthusiasm to welcome guests. As soon as they saw the travellers they jumped up and eagerly invited them into their home, offering them a meal and a place to sleep.

Admittedly, the accommodation was somewhat lacking because the people did not have very much. But whatever they had, they were willing to share, doing the best they could to observe the *mitzvah* of *hachnosas orchim*, showing hospitality to guests.

The following morning, the two travellers bade their hosts farewell and set out again. Shortly after they had departed, Rabbi Yehoshua ben Levi saw that Eliyahu HaNovi was praying. He listened closely. What was Eliyahu praying for? The elderly couple who had hosted them owned a cow. The cow was the most valuable possession they owned – indeed, the majority of their income came from the cow's milk. Eliyahu was praying that this cow should die.

When Rabbi Yehoshua heard this, he was shocked. The couple had been so nice, so pleasant, so warm. Why did they deserve that their cow should die? But he could not ask any questions. That was the agreement he had made.

As they proceeded on their journey, they talked. Rabbi Yehoshua hoped that Eliyahu would offer an explanation for what happened, or at least hint in that direction. But that was not so. Instead he directed the conversation to other issues. Toward evening, they came to a beautiful mansion. Although many members of the household saw them, no one offered them hospitality.

They asked the owner of the house, a very rich man, for permission to spend the night in his home. Reluctantly, the man agreed. But he was very cold to them, he did not offer any food and hardly said a word to them.

After they set off on their way in the morning, Rabbi Yehoshua noticed that Eliyahu was praying again. What was he praying for this time? One of the walls in this rich man's house was cracked and weak. Eliyahu was praying to G-d that this wall should be restored and should remain strong and solid.

Rabbi Yehoshua could not understand this. Here was a miser who had not acted kindly to them at all. And yet Eliyahu was praying for him, entreating G-d that his wall, which was cracked, should become solid and strong again. But once more, he abided by the terms of his agreement. No questions allowed.

Eventually, the two travellers arrived in a beautiful city; everything about the place reflected prosperity and opulence. They made their way to the *shule*. It was a magnificent structure, designed with elegance and taste. Everything, even the benches, was beautiful.

Rabbi Yehoshua ben Levi thought they would have no problem receiving hospitality in such a town. But it did not work out that way. The people were not very kind.

When the prayers were over, nobody approached them to ask where they planned to eat or where they were going to stay. Ultimately, they had to spend the night in the *shule*, sleeping on those beautiful benches without eating supper.

In the morning, when they were ready to leave, Eliyahu blessed the inhabitants of the city, wishing them that they should all become leaders. Again, Rabbi Yehoshua was puzzled. Why did Eliyahu bless people who had not shown them hospitality?

That evening, they came to another city. Obviously, it was not as wealthy a community as the first and the *shule* was nowhere near as beautiful. But the people were very fine, warm and kind. They did everything they could to make the two travellers comfortable. Before leaving that city, Eliyahu told them, 'May G-d help that only one of you becomes a leader.'

At this point, Rabbi Yehoshua could no longer contain his curiosity. He told Eliyahu, 'I know that by asking questions I will forfeit my right to accompany you, but I cannot go on like this. Please, explain these four incidents to me.'

And so Eliyahu began to explain: 'The elderly couple whom we met first, they were wonderful people who performed acts of great kindness. So I wanted to give them a blessing. It was destined for the woman to pass away that day, it was to be the last day of her life.

'But by hosting us, she was given the opportunity to perform a *mitzvah*. And the merit of the *mitzvah* of hospitality that she performed was great enough for the decree to be lifted, but not entirely. So I prayed that their cow – which meant so much to them and was their source of income – should die. Because the cow would die, the woman would have many more years to live. So the cow's death was really a blessing for them.

'About the miser's house. In that wall, a very great treasure lay buried. But the wall was weak and would soon break. Because he was a miser and conducted himself so crudely, I prayed that the wall should become strong so that he would not be able to benefit from the treasure.

'What about the people in the prosperous city?' Eliyahu continued. 'My prayer that they should all become leaders in the city is not a blessing; if anything, it is the opposite. For the most destructive thing that can happen in a city is that everybody becomes a leader.

In the other city, where the people were kind, I gave them a genuine blessing: that one, and only one, of them become a true leader.'

This story contains a lesson for all of us. Like Rabbi Yehoshua ben Levi, we have to realize that life is a large puzzle with many pieces, of which we possess only a small portion. So, of course we have questions. It is natural. For what we know about ourselves and about others is only a few pieces of a 5,000-piece puzzle. Is it any wonder that these few pieces do not seem to mean anything? The form of these pieces, the shape that results from their combination, does not look like anything, nor does it appear to lead to anything.

But that is because we have only a few pieces of a 5,000-piece puzzle. Once we receive the other four-thousand nine-hundred odd pieces and we add these few, everything falls into place and we see exactly how it fits in.

So we have to be patient and realize that we do not have the whole picture. Not about ourselves, about what happened before in our lives, what will happen later in our lives, about others in our community, or even about our parents and our children. And therefore, our vision is very limited and we do not understand many of the things we see.

THE FLOWER PLUCKED BY THE MASTER

Traditional story[52]

A gentleman's gardener had a darling girl whom he loved dearly. At a tender age she was fatally stricken. The father was terribly distressed.

In one of his flowerbeds the gardener had a favourite rose. It was the fairest flower he had ever seen on the tree and he daily marked its growing beauty, intending when it was in full bloom to send it to his master's mansion.

One morning, it was gone. Someone had plucked it.

Mortified at what he thought was the improper conduct of one of the servants, he tried to find out the culprit.

He was, however, much surprised that it was his master who, on walking through the garden, had been attracted by the beauty of the rose and plucking it had carried it to one of the beautiful rooms in the hall.

The gardener's anger was changed into pleasure. He felt reconciled when he heard that his master had thought the flower worthy of such special notice.

'Ah, Richard,' said the gentleman, 'you are happy to give up the rose because you see that it is worthy of a place in my home. Yet you mourn because G-d has thought it wise to remove your child from a world of trial and hardship to be with Him in heaven!'

---

[52] Originally written by Hudson Taylor, a British Protestant Christian missionary to China, in 1868, but elaborated on over the years.
http://www.worldinvisible.com/library/hudsontaylor/hudsontaylorv2/hudsontaylorv209.htm

PICK UP THE LOAD

Cheryl Mandel[53]

Daniel's army training was eighteen months long. His group of soldiers mark the end of the training with a ninety-kilometre trek. Not an easy trek, by any means. Much, much harder than you can even imagine.

Each soldier had been specifically trained. As well as marching in all their gear and provisions, the first-aid guy had all the first-aid equipment, the communications guy had all the radio equipment, and a real strong soldier had been trained to carry the machine gun, which weighed over six kilograms.

Very early into the walk, the burly soldier with the heavy machine gun collapsed. Daniel rushed over to him.

The Commanding Officer went up to Daniel and commanded him to pick up the machine gun.

Daniel wasn't trained to carry this heavy weapon. He wasn't strong enough to carry the machine gun, but he picked up that solid piece of equipment, put it on his back and walked.

And he walked and he walked and he walked until he finished that ninety-kilometre trek.

---

[53] Cheryl Mandel wrote this after her son Daniel Mandel *z"l* was killed in Israel in 2003. Daniel commanded a mission to hunt wanted terrorists. His team of soldiers from the elite commando unit of the Nachal Brigade succeeded in the mission he led, but Daniel was killed. Permission to include was obtained from Cheryl.

He was exhausted when he finished that walk, but he persevered because his Commanding Officer had told him to pick up the machine gun and walk, to continue the trek.

As a bereaved mother, I am also on a trek, a trek called life. And here in the middle of the trek, this arduous journey, I've been given this extra burden— this machine gun, this heavy, heavy load.

I haven't trained for it.

I'm not willing to take it. I'm not strong enough for it, but *Hashem*, my Commanding Officer, said, 'Cheryl, pick it up. Take this burden.' And I am trying to do this in the most positive way that I can, with dignity and love. I am doing it out of love for my son, Daniel.

THE DREAM

Cheryl Mandel[54]

Cheryl also related the story of a lady whose child had died. The mother was sad. She cried day and night, she cried night and day. She cried for weeks, she cried for months. She could not get herself together to stop crying.

Then one night she had a dream. In her dream she went down a long dark corridor. At the end of the corridor there was a door. She opened a door and entered a banquet room. It was full of beautiful young men and women. They were sitting around the table. They were laughing and singing. Some were eating and drinking. Some of them were studying.

Suddenly, in the corner, she saw her son. She ran to him and threw her arms around him and said, 'Sweetheart!', and she hugged him and kissed him. She could not stop hugging him and kissing him.

But then she said, 'Just a second. Why are you in the corner?

Why aren't you with the guys? Why aren't you having a good time?'

And he looked at her and he said, 'Mother, how can I be happy when you are so sad?'

---

[54] Taken from a speech given by Cheryl Mandel at the Israeli Consulate in New York in April 2017
https://www.youtube.com/watch?v=Wx8roMpTFgc

THE WORST THAT COULD HAPPEN

A traditional story[55]

One day Jacob ran into the rabbi's study.

'Rabbi, it's terrible. My ox died. Now I won't be able to plough my field. Isn't this the worst thing that could possibly happen to me?'

'Maybe it is, maybe it isn't,' answered the rabbi.

The next day, Jacob again ran into the rabbi's house. 'Rabbi, it is wonderful. Yesterday, on my way home, I found a beautiful horse walking in the forest. With the horse I ploughed my field twice as fast as I used to with my ox. Isn't this the best thing that could possibly happen to me?'

'Maybe it is, maybe it isn't', answered the rabbi.

The next day, Jacob again ran into the rabbi's house. 'Rabbi, it is terrible. My son fell off his new horse and broke both his legs. Isn't this the worst thing that could possibly happen to me?'

'Maybe it is, maybe it isn't', answered the rabbi.

The next day, soldiers of the king came to Jacob's village. They took away all the boys and forced them into the

---

[55] To the best of my recollection I came across this story in a *shule* or community newsletter. However, in trying to find a source on the internet I found references to a version accredited to Zen Buddhism as well as a similar version in the book *Don't sweat the small stuff … and it's all small stuff*, by Robert Carlson and a more relevant version in *My first book of Jewish stories* by Shmuel Blitz

king's army. The only boy not taken was Jacob's son, because both his legs were broken.

Now Jacob understood the rabbi's wise words. We don't always understand what G-d does, but everything He does is for the best.

THE PURPOSE OF PRAYER

Shira Bloch Wenig[56]

A lot of our prayers deal with our needs and desires. We ask *Hashem* for health, wisdom, economic prosperity, redemption, the rebuilding of Jerusalem and so on. Of course we praise *Hashem* and thank Him for everything He does for us, but much of the time we're asking for things we need – almost like we're giving *Hashem* a shopping list to be delivered to our doorstep. At first glance, this sounds quite selfish, as though we *daven* so that we can get what we want.

This view of prayer is not only superficial, it's misleading. What about when we don't get the answer we want? Does that mean we didn't *daven* properly? *Tefillah* is not about getting what we want. It's not about saying the right words and getting blessings delivered on a silver platter, just like putting the right coins in a vending machine and waiting for a Coke to pop out.

Tefillah is not about getting results. It's about us simple human beings entering into a conversation with *Hashem*. Judaism describes it as a connection between the finite and the divine.

Rav Yosef Dov Soloveitchik points out that we communicate with *Hashem* through a dialogue. When G-d speaks to man, that's prophecy. We don't have direct prophecy anymore. We do have the *Torah, Hashem*'s direct word, and the ability to study it. The other side of the conversation is when man speaks to G-d, and that's

---

56 This is a copy of the speech given by Shira Bloch Wenig at a 2013 Siddur concert at Beth Rivkah Ladies College, held annually in memory of her sister Yael. Permission to include obtained from Shira.

---

tefillah. It's incredible to realise that every single one of us, no matter how old or young, learned or not, has an open invitation to approach the Creator of the World and initiate our own conversation with Him.

Tefillah does contain a lot of requests. We see examples of this all through *Tanach.* Eliezer *davened* to *Hashem* to help him find a suitable wife for Yitzchak. Yaakov prayed to G-d to save him from his brother Esav. Moshe *davened* for his sister Miriam to be cured of leprosy and Chana prayed for a son. We too are advised in *Pirkei Avot* not to make our prayers mundane and repetitive, but to include an element of pleading. So what's the point of this?

Making requests is a recognition of the fact that everything we need comes from *Hashem.* Our existence is totally dependent on G-d and it's only through approaching Him that we can find comfort. Whether or not *Hashem* grants us what we ask for, the value is in the conversation itself. We can draw strength and faith from going right to the source and talking to *Hashem*, who is our only real port of call.

It's easy to remember the many *tefillot* (prayers) which were not answered in the way we desperately wanted. But we should also remember all the *tefillot* which continue to be answered with blessings in abundance.

May your conversations with *Hashem* be a source of strength and fulfilment for you.

KADDISH

Rabbi Raymond Apple[57]

WHAT IS THE ORIGIN OF *KADDISH YATOM*, THE MOURNER'S *KADDISH*?

Despite the popular view, *Kaddish* did not begin as a mourner's prayer and *Kaddish Yatom* is only one version of *Kaddish*. The *Kaddish* is an amalgam of phrases commencing with a passage from Ezekiel 28:33. When the people are in exile, says Ezekiel, G-d will ensure that His Presence is revealed: 'I will magnify Myself and sanctify Myself *(v'hitgaddalti v'hitkaddashti)* and I will make Myself known in the eyes of many nations, and they shall know that I am the Lord'. These Divine words were adapted to become *yitgaddal v'yitkaddash* ('May He be magnified and sanctified') and to express our faith that the redemption will come.

The *Kaddish* prays that G-d's kingdom may come 'in your life and in your days and in the life of all the House of Israel' implying, according to the medieval authority Abudarham, 'May the redemption not be delayed and may it come without birth pangs.' The congregational response to the first paragraph, *Y'hei sh'mei rabba* ('May His great name be blessed forever'), is highly emphasised by the sages and whoever says it is assured of a place in the World to Come (Shab. 57a).

---

57 Rabbi Dr Raymond Apple, previously the Senior Rabbi of the Great Synagogue of Sydney Shule, now resides in Israel. Permission to include obtained from him.

According to *Talmudic* sources, *Kaddish* was recited by a preacher after his sermon or a scholar after his discourse

.

None of this material suggests a link with mourning, but Rabbi DS Telsner, in his *The Kaddish - Its History and Significance* (ed. GA Sivan, Jerusalem, 1995), puts forward the idea that the development of the mourner's version of the *Kaddish* may have come about as the result of a shift in emphasis. At first the *Kaddish* honoured the living ('in your life and in your days'). During the medieval persecutions it consoled the survivors of catastrophes and implied that they should not let their tragic experiences weaken their faith in redemption. Eventually, it memorialised those who had lost their lives and so it became a prayer for the dead rather than the living.

This theory reflects the fact that the mourner's *Kaddish* probably arose in north-west and central Europe in the Middle Ages. Another medieval source, the *Machzor Vitry*, speaks of a mourner conducting the service on Saturday night, probably because of the belief that at the end of *Shabbat* the dead are selected either for punishment or for reward. Eventually the mourners recited *Kaddish* without necessarily conducting the service, and finally, *Kaddish* at the end of the service became the mourner's prerogative.

ON CHILDREN

Kahlil Gibran[58]

Your children are not your children.
They are the sons and daughters of Life's longing for
itself.
They come through you but not from you,
And though they are with you yet they belong not to you.

You may give them your love but not your thoughts,
For they have their own thoughts.
You may house their bodies but not their souls,
For their souls dwell in the house of tomorrow,
which you cannot visit, not even in your dreams.
You may strive to be like them,
but seek not to make them like you.
For life goes not backward nor tarries with yesterday.

You are the bows from which your children
as living arrows are sent forth.
The archer sees the mark upon the path of the infinite,
and He bends you with His might
that His arrows may go swift and far.
Let your bending in the archer's hand be for gladness;
For even as He loves the arrow that flies,
so He loves also the bow that is stable.

---

[58] Khalil Gibran was a Lebanese-American poet, writer, artist and
philosopher. He died in 1931. The poetic essay is from his book *The
Prophet.* See – https://en.wikipedia.org/wiki/Kahlil_Gibran

THE FIG TREE

A story from the *Midrash*[59]

Rabbi Akiva and his students used to sit and study under a fig tree, whose owner would get up early every morning and gather fruit from this tree.

The students began to suspect that the owner rose up early each day to pluck the fruit so they would not take figs for themselves. The students therefore decided to sit elsewhere.

When the owner of the tree finally found them, he said: 'Why would you deprive me of having the credit of you studying under my tree? I never suspected you of taking the fruit! I got up early each morning to gather the fruit because once the sun comes out, the figs become wormy.'

The next morning, the owner of the fig tree did not come to pluck the fruit and sure enough, the students found the fruit was spoiled by the heat of the sun.

The *Midrash* concludes that *Hashem*, like the tree owner, knows when is the right time to summon his children to return to Him.

---

[59] From *Akiva* by Marcus Lehmann, Feldheim Publishers

<u>SOME REVIEWS OF THIS BOOK</u>

I've have read select parts of your book, particularly the part about G-d. In addition to the fact that you write well, the content of what you've written is very real. It is obviously confronting, and I suspect those who read it and have not lost a child will view the relationships they do have quite differently. I certainly will.

A central theme I sensed that runs through your book is the notion of acceptance. To accept the new reality. This doesn't mean forgetting about the past and certainly not being content with the present (as you say several times you remain angry with G-d, which is entirely justified) but to simply find a space within your soul to come to terms with the loss of a child.

Additionally, your very sensitive approach towards mental illness and suicide was most enlightening and I agree with you that parents of children who took their lives struggle severely with a sense of guilt, perhaps more so than those who lost a child from illness. Yet, as you point out, the last thing those parents need is for society to label their children as having 'committed' suicide, as if to say they've done something deliberately wrong. Severe depression can be debilitating, and I think you spell this out very candidly in your book.

Overall, I genuinely believe your book will make a huge difference to the lives of parents going through the despair and grief of losing a child. I think the fact that they will see in you someone who has travelled the same path they are travelling (as opposed to a book from a psychologist or therapist, of which there are many) will add enormous credibility and gravitas to the messages you are conveying. Overall, I must take my hat off to you.

It was no doubt a daunting and challenging task, but I feel you have achieved your goal with distinction.

Thank you again for sharing a copy with me and for the privilege of providing you a letter of support which now has even more meaning in my own heart, having read what I did.

Rabbi Yaakov Glasman, Senior Rabbi, St Kilda Synagogue

I just finished reading your book. I can't believe how you have captured so much. It's made me realise that I am 'normal' and what I feel is ok. It will be invaluable to people who are just beginning this traumatic journey. I found great comfort in your chapter on reincarnation. It made me feel that Natalie is in a safe place and we will meet again. Wish I had read it all months ago.

HL, bereaved mother of Natalie, 1970 - 2017

What a beautiful, heartfelt expression of personal grief and practical grieving. Cynthia's open and honest sharing of her experience of the loss of her son, Danny, as well as her exploration of the loss of a child experienced by others, provides a sense of grounding and comfort for those who find themselves in this dreadful situation. Losing a child is not the natural order of things. Nothing can prepare us. As Cynthia rightly notes, every parent both experiences and expresses their loss differently. Creating a resource for Jewish parents to help provide a context for the plethora of emotional, physical, and ritual responses, enables parents a point of reference and access to a community of parents who share their pain. This book is a reminder that they are not alone and that, although time does not heal all wounds, time brings a return to the world, to life again.

This is an incredibly powerful resource for parents dealing with the unthinkable loss of their child, as well as anyone supporting others dealing with loss. There is no quick fix or easy way through the process of grief. This book is a formidable companion for those who walk this road. Thank you, Cynthia for sharing your story, your journey, your strength and your wisdom.

Rabbi Allison Conyer, Etz Chayim Progressive Synagogue

The death of a child is a frightening, isolating and an overwhelming experience. For many bereaved parents caught in this maelstrom of strong emotions the ability to connect with another person, either through engagement in a bereavement support group or through reading the stories of others who have experienced and survived similar losses, can provide a soothing balm amid their distress.

Cynthia has used her skills and motivation to bring the wisdom garnered from this group context, along with the experience of her own painful loss, to bear in this new book which addresses many of the common fears and issues confronted by bereaved parents. What makes this book remarkable is that it directly addresses the virtual absence of books and literature which speak directly to the bereaved Jewish parent.

We know that the search for meaning is often a central task for the bereaved person. For those with a spiritual or religious belief these questions can become a central concern. Cynthia's book speaks eloquently to the needs of all Jewish bereaved parents. Just as Cynthia has had a profound impact on the lives of bereaved Jewish parents through the establishment of a dedicated support program, I believe that this book equally has the capacity to speak directly to the hearts and minds of those who read it. This book will certainly be of relevance and a critically important resource for Jewish bereaved parents, but also more widely because it speaks to the universal issues of love, loss and bereavement.

Christopher Hall, CEO, Australian Centre for Grief and Bereavement
(Phone 03 9265 2100)

As a Jewish bereaved parent and a specialist grief and loss counsellor I found Cynthia's book a beautiful read for those who have experienced the death of their child.

Grief is often considered an incredibly lonely journey, a journey that no one else can really understand...no matter how hard they try. Cynthia's book offers beautiful words of companionship, of knowingness, wisdom and understanding. The easy to follow sections allow the reader to pick it up and put it down as their questions arise.

Through the reading of this book the reader will be consistently reassured that they are not going mad and that what they are experiencing is normal. The focus on Jewish rituals and customs also provides a framework for both the grieving person and the people trying to support them.

It is rare to find a book written by a bereaved parent that covers the theoretical principles of grief, whilst maintaining the warmth and integrity of the writer's personal story within the context of the Jewish religion. I would happily give the book to my clients to read.

Karen Ludski, M Couns BA (Psych); Dip Prof Couns; Grad Dip Couns Supervision; Grad Cert Ber Couns (Phone 03 9500 8381)

Cynthia has woven a complex tapestry in this book. Her ability to offer and share with the reader insight into her own personal story, her internal struggles and emotions while at the same time providing perspective, knowledge and resources on this painful topic is certainly unique. Having stood side by side with parents who were grieving the loss of their child and seeing the devastation it caused them I think having this book available as a resource for them will be invaluable. Although no two people experience or express loss in the same way, the truly empathic, openness and non-judgemental approach of this book will no doubt be helpful for parents and provide an "additional hand" for parents to hold as they navigate life after loss.

I also think this book is an excellent resource for anyone working with or supporting those who have lost a child. Cynthia has been able to open a small window for us to look through and get a brief glimpse into their world and I have personally learned a lot from reading this book. I would strongly recommend communal rabbis to read this book and to have it available to share with their congregants if ever needed.

The book is structured in a way that it covers the many stages, difficulties and challenges that arise after the loss of a child and this could be reassuring for parents in understanding their own journey. I also found her overview of the Jewish customs and traditions around mourning very useful and there is an excellent selection of inspirational readings at the end of the book.

I would like to thank Cynthia for this beautiful resource and for her willingness to use her own experience to assist others.

Rabbi Daniel Rabin, Rabbi South Caulfield Hebrew Congregation
Master of Counselling and Psychotherapy

When reading Cynthia's book, I felt a strong connection with her thoughts and feelings. It has been over ten years since my beloved son, Michael, died and I have read many books about the death of a child. This book however is by far the most factual, warm, sensitive and informative that I have read. I cried and laughed and gained much from Cynthia's experiences and interesting and thought-provoking stories. I would have greatly appreciated and benefited from a book such as this when Michael died.

I would highly recommend this book to anyone whose child has died recently or many years ago.

AF, bereaved mother of Michael, 1974 – 2007

The most important message Cynthia Pollak conveys in her volume, *After the death of your child, a Jewish mother's perspective* is "I am living" – at times the hardest thing to do after your child dies. The death of a child changes one forever. Grief is a process that one learns to live with, not to recover from or get over. In the living after the death of a child, relationships change, identity changes, responsibility changes. Cynthia weaves the psychological evidence into her story, in a way that will assist parents who have lost a child and those who wish to support them. Her acknowledgement of the particular challenges and resources that being Jewish and a grieving parent bring with them will help Jewish people connect and feel heard.

Thank you for reminding us all of the value of community. Thank you for ensuring that the Jewish community of Australia is truly one, and that all who have lost a child can be comforted. Support groups run by and for those who have lost a child are the source of great strength and are needed wherever there are parents, as there will always be losses. But we who are blessed with living children need to better understand the pain of the loss and do more to support the grieving parents among us. Cynthia's book should help us do better.

Associate Professor Amanda Gordon, Director, Armchair Psychology
Founding President, Chessed Bereavement Support Services, Sydney

(Phone 02 9362 3490)

An engaging, informative and touching book. Up-to-date and very accessible in style of writing and short chapters with itemised sub-sections. Great to read about and get a sense of Danny, too.

Andrew McNess, CEO, The Compassionate Friends of Victoria
(Phone 03 9888 4944)

This is a personal story about what it is like to be a bereaved Jewish parent, it is written from the heart and full of emotion. Cynthia has included beautiful quotes throughout her book that add weight to her feelings. I liked the Guideposts section that provides simple and useful hints to cope with grieving. Most of all I like that she addressed a question most bereaved parents dread, 'How many children do you have?'

While this book is for Jewish bereaved parents, I found it extremely informative and it provided me with a glimpse of the Jewish faith and customs around grieving. As a counsellor I would be happy to recommend this book to my clients.

**Susan Meyerink, Specialist Bereavement Counsellor,
Melbourne
(Phone 0425 692 555)**

www.ingramcontent.com/pod-product-compliance
Lightning Source LLC
Chambersburg PA
CBHW071408150726
48000CB00001B/219